Stage Fright in Music Performance and Its Relationship to the Unconscious

STAGE FRIGHT IN MUSIC PERFORMANCE AND ITS RELATIONSHIP TO THE UNCONSCIOUS

SECOND EDITION

MICHAEL I. GOODE

TRUMPETWORKS PRESS

OAK PARK, ILLINOIS

Trumpetworks Press, 715 Lake Street #269, Oak Park, Illinois 60301
Copyright © 2002, 2003 by Michael Ian Goode
All rights reserved. Protected Under the Berne Convention
First edition published 2002. Second edition 2003
Printed in the United States of America

Nothing in this book should be taken as medical advice. For any specific problems you should consult your physician.

All of the case histories found in this book are composites derived from many performers in the field of music. Any resemblance to any one particular living or deceased individual is unintended and is purely coincidental. This book is printed on acid-free, recycled paper.

Library of Congress Cataloging-in-Publication Data

Goode, Michael.
   Stage fright in music performance and its relationship to the unconscious / Michael I. Goode.--2nd ed.
      p. cm.
   Includes bibliographic references and index.
   ISBN 0-9743934-1-X (alk. paper)
      1. Music--Performance – Psychological aspects. 2. Music – Performance – Physiological aspects. 3. Stage fright. I. Title.

ML3830.G66 2003
781.4'3111--dc22

2003053400

To Wendy, The Love of My Life

EVERYTHING COMES FROM THE MIND

CONTENTS

ILLUSTRATIONS

TABLES

PREFACE TO THE SECOND EDITION

Although the material in this text, based on my thesis from the University of Chicago, has already been published, there were too many requests, so it was necessary to publish a second, paperback edition. This edition includes this preface and additional photographs from the author's professional career. These photographs should enhance the reader's perception of life in the professional music world by providing actual examples of some of the persons and professional situations mentioned in the text.

Due to many inquiries, this second edition also includes additional textual material related to the author's professional career. An article "Physiological Effects of Rebreathing of CO_2 in Trumpet-Playing," has been included as an addition to the original text. This article elaborates on a specific aspect of playing the trumpet, and will hopefully help the reader to gain additional insight into the author's experience as a professional trumpet player which is crucial in understanding the original text.

I sincerely hope that this work will stimulate you to think about the issue of stage fright and its relationship to the unconscious in not only a musical context, but in a much broader way.

Preface to the Second Edition

ACKNOWLEDGEMENTS

I am indebted to Will Scarlett and Adolph Herseth of the Chicago Symphony Orchestra, my thesis advisor Philip Hoffmann of the University of Chicago, Biological Sciences Division, Donald Greene of the Julliard School of Music, the late Arnold Jacobs of the Chicago Symphony Orchestra, and Paul Renard, pianist and music theorist, for their help and their wealth of information regarding this topic.

Many thanks also to Joseph Lee for lending me material, for his insights into health and medicine, and for his interest in my work. And many thanks also to Lori Weiss, M.D., for her help and suggestions. To Kathleen Heller, thanks for your fabulous proofreading work.

In addition, thanks go to the Master of Liberal Arts Program of the Graham School for General Studies at the University of Chicago for being invaluable in providing the scholarly background for such an endeavor.

Thanks to Jennie and Lior Azoulai, and Cheryl Marzolf for their support. To my colleague Mike Lanier, thanks for your encouragement on this topic.

Thanks to Randy Waldman, and his parents Burt and Charna, who always believed I could do anything musically. And to O. D. Premo, who believed the same.

And finally, thanks to my wife Wendy, without whom this work would not have been possible.

INTRODUCTION

The study of classical music, voice, and their performance have been the subject of many books and magazine articles. Many of these writings discuss the rules of etiquette, protocol, and musical style with regard to performance of musical works in the orchestral and vocal field. However, very few have touched on the role of the unconscious in music performance.

There are both positive and negative aspects of the role of the unconscious in the performance of music. The positive aspects result in a joyous, memorable performance, and the negative aspects result in a disastrous, uncomfortable experience for both the audience, and even more so, for the performer. When performers cannot display their musical talent to their highest level of ability in front of an audience, it is most likely that they are suffering from performance anxiety, more commonly known as stage fright.

There are underlying psychological reasons for the condition of stage fright and its potentially devastating effects. These reasons can also be described in physiological and biochemical terms. We will discuss present medical and other solutions to this problem.

All of the case histories found in this book are composites derived from many performers in the field of music. Any resemblance to any one particular living or deceased individual is unintended and is purely coincidental.

ABBREVIATIONS

CNS   Central Nervous System

EP   Epinephrine

HR   Heart Rate

NE   Norepinephrine

PNS   Peripheral Nervous System

A Note To The Reader

The citation system used in this text is one that is currently in vogue among the social sciences and other faculty at the University of Chicago. Rather than the traditional footnote system, this system simply puts the author's name followed by the year and page number of the cited work at the end of the relevant text or section.

For example: (Copland, 1953, 23); would represent a reference on page 23 of the following work listed in the bibliography at the end of the main text:

Copland, Aaron. *What to Listen for in Music.* New York: Mentor Books, 1953.

This way, you can simply find the related text in the bibliography and look up the reference at a later point. There are a handful of traditional footnotes in the main text that are not bibliographic in nature. Due to its brevity, the article that serves as the *Appendix to the Second Edition* uses traditional endnotes.

1

OVERVIEW

The study of music and its performance has been the subject of many books and magazine articles. Most of these writings discuss the rules of etiquette, protocol, and musical style with regard to performance of musical works in the orchestral field. However, very few have touched on stage fright in music performance and its relationship to the unconscious.

For the purposes of this book, I will explore the area of orchestral music, sometimes referred to colloquially as "classical" music. Even though the term "classical music" technically refers to a period and not a specific field of music, I will use it to refer to orchestral music. I will also provide some examples in the area of operatic singing.

I will focus in this work on mine and my colleagues' performance experience in orchestral wind instruments and voice, and will specifically speak about the trumpet with regard to my own experience and other instruments when referring to the experiences of my colleagues. It is important to note, however, that the concepts discussed here could easily be applied to any instrument in the orchestral family, brass, woodwinds, percussion, or strings, as well as the voice.

A detailed discussion of these families and the various instruments within them is not germane to the concepts in this text. Any of the personal histories given in this thesis are based on my own research, observations, and interviews. Names and details have been changed and composite characters have been created, where necessary, to ensure anonymity. Although such discussion may not be relevant to this thesis, the concepts presented within the scope of this work regarding stage fright may be applied to any performance activity, including acting, athletics, or even a corporate presentation.

In this work I will propose a method by which the condition of stage fright can be identified and corrected using the above fields of music for my illustrative examples.

DEFINITIONS

Stage fright is a "nervous and physiological condition in which normally competent functioning necessary for successful completion of the situation is impaired."[1] The degree of stage fright depends on the degree of impairment. The impairment may be physiological, psychological, or spiritual. This condition is common to any area of public performance. In severe cases, stage fright can occur even in the preparation period for such a performance. Stage fright is also known as "performance anxiety" (Greene, *Fight Your Fear,* 2001, vi).

Performance is: "any activity done in front of any audience."[2] Using this definition of performance, areas other than music could be considered in this study. Among those areas are public speaking, acting, and athletics. But as mentioned above in the definitions of performance anxiety and in the discussions of case histories, we are going to limit ourselves to examples from music.

BRIEF MEDICAL DESCRIPTION OF STAGE FRIGHT

Stage fright is directly associated with fear (Fredrikson and Gunnarsson 1992, 51-52).

Some of the characteristics of stage fright are an increase in heart rate, an increase in the excretion of both epinephrine and cortisol, and a change in the excretion of norepinephrine (Ibid.). This change of norepinephrine excretion varies due to the degree of stage fright (Ibid.). Other characteristics are confused thinking, sweating, muscle tremor, dry mouth, nausea, and hyperventilation (Greene, *Fight Your Fear,* 2001, 47-48).

Both   epinephrine   and   norepinephrine   are   classified   as catecholamines (Goodman and Gilman, 2001, 215) and are produced in the medulla part of the adrenal gland, located on top of the

---

1This is my definition for the purposes of this work.
[2] Ibid.

kidneys as well as in the central and peripheral nervous systems (Rothenberg, 2000, 104). "Norepinephrine is the major neurotransmitter for the peripheral sympathetic nervous system" (Goodman and Gilman, 2001, 215).

Coordinated motions and feelings of the body are controlled by the central nervous system (CNS), which is composed of the brain and the spinal cord (Rothenberg, 2000, 108-9) (Fig. 1). The peripheral nervous system (PNS) is a network of nerves that extends to all the extremities of the body (Ibid., 433). The PNS sends signals to and from the CNS, controlling all voluntary actions and sensory perceptions (Ibid.). The individual nerve cells, or neurons, carry electrical impulses away via their axons, and impulses are carried towards them via structures known as dendrites (Ibid., 389). Sensory neurons involved with feelings transmit impulses to the CNS, and motor neurons transmit impulses from the CNS to the muscles and glands (Ibid.).

These impulses can be transmitted between either two neurons or between a neuron and muscular tissue or gland cells (Ibid., 536). On an electron microscopic level, these impulses are transmitted via the action of neurotransmitting chemicals, or neurotransmitters (Eccles 1990, 3773), such as norepinephrine mentioned above. The impulse sites are known as synapses (Fig. 2), first proposed by Sherrington in 1906 (Sherrington, 1906, 17). Within these sites, the neurotransmitting chemicals are released from presynaptic nerve terminals (Eccles, 1990, 3774) (Fig. 3), bulb-like structures at the end of nerve axons called boutons (Ibid., 3773-4; Rothenberg, 2000, 82), into a structure called the synaptic cleft (Eccles, 1990, 3774). Such chemical transmission is happening continuously.

Such chemical transmission by the neurotransmitting chemicals described in the process above, are the basis of how we act, think, and feel (Panksepp, 1990, 45). In musicians, the processes of acting, thinking, and feeling are developed to a high level of artistic sophistication in both practice and performance (Frederiksen, 1996, 135-139). Stage fright interferes with this artistic process (Ibid., 159, Fredrikson[3] and Gunnarsson, 1992, 58).

---

[3] Frederiksen, Brian, (first mentioned), and Fredrikson, Mats are two different people. The first is a tuba player and was Arnold Jacobs' personal assistant, and the second is from the Department of Psychology at Stockholm University in Sweden. It is sheer coincidence that they have nearly the same surname. They are not related in any way, nor do they know each other.

THE CENTRAL NERVOUS SYSTEM

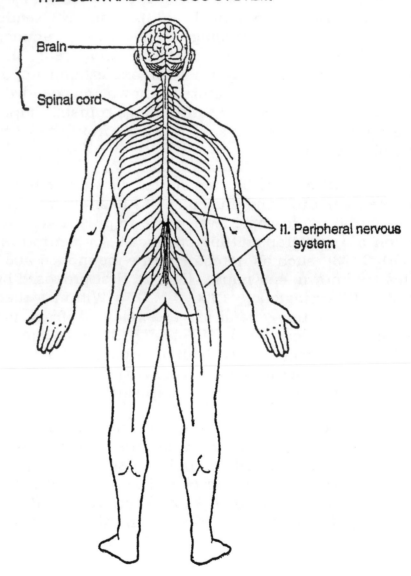

Fig 1. Diagram of the Peripheral and Central Nervous Systems (PNS) and (CNS) from *Dictionary of Medical Terms*, 4th edition by Mikel A. Rothenberg, and Charles F. Chapman. Copyright © 2000 by Barron's Educational Series, Inc. Reprinted by arrangement with Barron's Educational Series, Inc.

The Journal of Neuroscience, December 1990, *10*(12) 3773

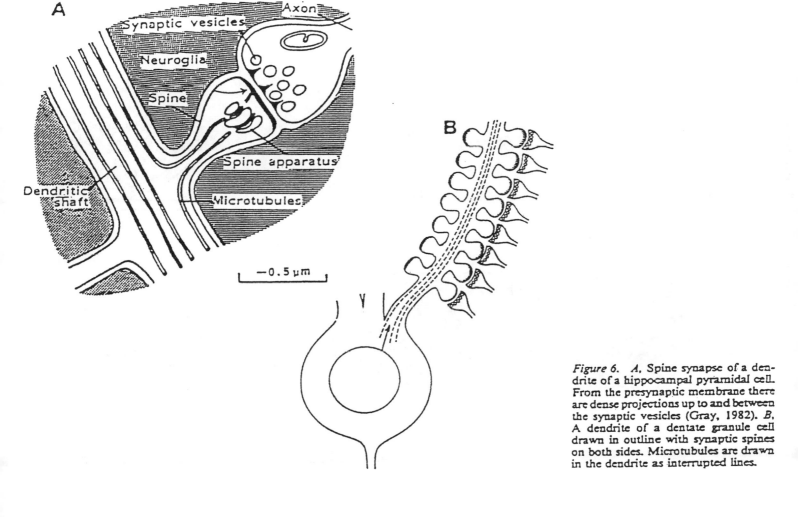

Figure 6. A, Spine synapse of a dendrite of a hippocampal pyramidal cell. From the presynaptic membrane there are dense projections up to and between the synaptic vesicles (Gray, 1982). *B*, A dendrite of a dentate granule cell drawn in outline with synaptic spines on both sides. Microtubules are drawn in the dendrite as interrupted lines.

Fig. 2.   Synapse, from Eccles, John C., "Developing Concepts of the Synapses." *The Journal of Neuroscience* 10 (12) (December 1990): 3773. Diagrams courtesy of the Society for Neuroscience. © 1990 by the Society for Neuroscience.

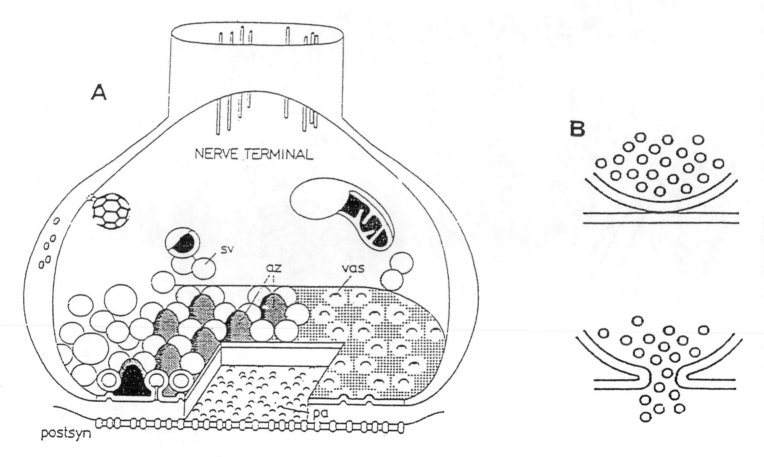

3774 Eccles • Developing Concepts of the Synapses

Figure 7. *A,* Schema of the mammalian central synapse. The active zone (*AZ*) is formed by presynaptic dense projections. *SV,* Synaptic vesicles; *PA,* particle aggregation on postsynaptic membrane (*postsyn.*). Note synaptic vesicles in hexagonal array on the left and vesicle attachment sites (*VAS*) on the right (Akert et al., 1975). *B,* Stages of exocytosis with release of transmitter into the synaptic cleft.

Fig. 3.   Synapse, from Eccles, John C., "Developing Concepts of the Synapses."
The Journal of Neuroscience 10 (12) (December 1990): 3774. Diagrams courtesy of
the Society for Neuroscience. © 1990 by the Society for Neuroscience.

SOLUTIONS

There are many proposed solutions to the problem of stage fright. Some of these solutions are medical, some are strictly psychological, and others are more traditionally orientated but can be described on a physiological and neurobiochemical basis. We will discuss these various solutions and their benefits in Chapter 3 in some detail. But before we do this, we are now going to present some composite case histories of persons with varying degrees of stage fright. Four cases will be presented: Rolf, Stacy, Jimmy, and Bobby, with Bobby serving as our control case.

2

CASE HISTORIES

ROLF – ORCHESTRAL

Let us examine the case of a student named Rolf. Rolf is 38 years old and plays trombone. He has been trained by some of the finest teachers and has attended a prestigious music school as a music minor, but has an enormous amount of natural talent, which has been duly noted by his famous teachers from the New York Philharmonic. His teachers constantly encourage him, but he still cannot pass any major symphonic auditions because of his stage fright. He works very hard, and yet such success eludes him because every time he takes an audition, he fails miserably. When Rolf plays at auditions for large, prestigious orchestras, he especially fails because he gets so nervous that his playing breaks down during the audition.

MUSICAL CAREER

Rolf started playing the trombone at age 10 while in the fourth grade. He was very excited as a child about the trumpet, but on the first day of band class, his band director instructed him that he would be playing the trombone instead. Rolf argued, but it was of no use. The band director had grounded his decision on certain pedagogical theories at the time that were based strictly on body structure and facial and dental characteristics. These theories stated that there is a certain physiological characteristic, a physical type, for every instrument (Wolfe, 1964, 1). According to such pedagogy, thin lips and straight teeth are needed for the trumpet, average lips and an overbite, for the clarinet, and large thick lips and straight teeth for the trombone and/or tuba (Ibid.).

The band director's decision crushed little Rolf, and he was very disappointed. His heroes had been Louis Armstrong, the founder of jazz (Hadley, 1980, 421), and Adolph Herseth of the Chicago Symphony, and now he was no longer going to be able to play the trumpet. But, he did love music and wanted to play, even if it was not the instrument he wanted. Perhaps he could play the trumpet some day.

So, little Rolf plays the trombone. This is much to the anger and dismay of his parents and his brother. Even though his father had been given an old trombone from a coworker, he does not like music or musicians. Apparently, some distant great-uncle, who had been a professional musician in Europe, had a reputation as a ne'er-do-well. The prejudice from this family history was displaced entirely upon little Rolf (Rothenberg, 2000, 156) quite unfairly. The family complains that his playing is too loud, tells him to "go play in the garage," "we will send you to the garage!" and finally screams at him, "why don't you just quit?"[1]

But, little Rolf is determined. He continues to play and he loves music. Unfortunately, the band director is still upset that Rolf tried to argue his way into playing the trumpet instead of the trombone. As punishment for this seeming insubordination, the band director always makes Rolf sit last chair in the elementary school band, in spite of the fact that Rolf actually plays quite well for his age. This punishment is devastating to the little boy (Lavatelli, 1970, 5).

So little Rolf pretty much has to go it alone, in his practice room, besieged by both of his parents and his brother, and at school, he gets nothing but meanness from the band director. But Rolf plays on. He listens to records at home, and plays the trombone at his friend's house. His friend's parents are kind and very interested in both their son's, and Rolf's music making.

So what has happened here? At this stage, although there are some positive elements in the relationship between Rolf, his friend, and his friend's family, the rest of his world relating to music is overwhelmingly negative. The messages that Rolf is receiving from his immediate family, the ones who matter most to him (Lavatelli,

---

[1] This quote is taken, verbatim, with permission, from one of the interview subjects whose history is part of this case history.

1970, 5), make him feel like he is a bad person, crazy to be doing music, and that he is making his parents and brother angry. Rolf begins to feel that he is a bad person for doing music.

In the back of his mind, in his subconscious (Rothenberg, 2000, 531), he is asking himself these questions: "Why am I doing something that makes my parents and brother angry with me? And why are my friend's parents nice to me and encourage my music while my parents and brother oppose it? Is there something wrong with me? Is there something wrong with music, or doing music? Why is music fun at my friend's house and not at home? Why do my parents and brother scream so much at me when I practice?" Rolf feels very stressed and insecure within his own home. He is socially separated from the members of his family because of their hostility towards music, and this causes a form of stress within him known as separation distress (Panksepp, 1990, 47). This stress will seriously impact his physiological health as time goes on (Ibid.).

For performers and musical artists to play at the highest level, they must be secure in what they are doing in order to achieve a successful performance, whether in an audition or in the concert hall (Greene, *Fight Your Fear*, 2001, 72-73). Musical artists must make a statement, tell a story when they play, they must be sure (Frederiksen, 1996, 136). Without this surety, this confidence, there is no artistry, at the highest level, only disaster, only failure that destroys one's confidence (Greene, *Fight Your Fear*, 2001, 72-73).

With the kind of questions little Rolf is asking himself in his formative years, his neurological patterns are beginning to be established, and are becoming inexorably linked to his physiology and his mental and emotional areas (Lavatelli, 1970, 5, and Panksepp, 1990, 45). The neurological patterns that are being formed are stress patterns, anxiety patterns, that are "fight-or-flight" in nature, rather than ones of happiness and security, like the ideal example given above (Ibid.). These patterns are difficult, but not impossible to break. Even if a performer becomes successful at the highest levels, a lack of full resolution of these stress patterns, developed in childhood, will cause the stress effect to remain buried in their unconscious and physiology (Ibid. and Lavatelli, 1970, 5).

Rolf goes on through his elementary school years, not yet having private lessons on his instrument, because his parents refuse to spend the money for a private instructor. He is forced to depend solely on the opinion of his band director for an evaluation of his personal progress on the instrument. Rolf pretty much ignores the very positive feedback of his friend's family towards his playing and music in general. He ignores these positive affirmations as a way of resolving the conflict between his parent's and brother's negative attitudes towards his trombone-playing and music, versus his friend's family's positive attitude. Rolf is forced to focus on the negative in order to maintain homeostatic balance within his negative environment in order to cope with his "state of homeostatic disequilibrium" on both an emotional and neurochemical basis (Panksepp, 1990, 45). His focus on negative behavior is one of his attempts to establish re-equilibrium in his brain chemistry (Ibid.). We will focus on more of these medical aspects later.

Rolf somehow progresses through junior high under a new band director. He is playing well, but not thinking anything much of it, just assuming that he must be a bad trombone player and a bad person. Much to Rolf's confusion, the junior high band director continues to have him play the first part and all the solos. He certainly says nothing to his parents about what he is doing in band, as he knows that too much discussion of what is going on will cause a violently negative reaction from them that could lead to a decision by them to pull him out of band altogether.

Although Rolf is trying to pretend and ignore the fact that he is actually playing well, in order to maintain his emotional and biochemical balance (Panksepp, 1990, 45), he has enough positive things going for him in his playing so that he can continue to progress. These positive events will keep him going in music, but will also continue to create conflict and raise questions about playing music. Arnold Jacobs, the eminent tubist of the Chicago Symphony Orchestra, said that "when making music, you should be making statements, not questions" (Jacobs, 1994-1996). It is this building inner conflict getting internalized that will cause Rolf to have a severe case of stage fright in his musical future.

The unconscious considers questions asked in the context of performance as stress reactions that put the performer in a "fight-or-flight" state, rather than in the optimum relaxed and alert state totally necessary for the highest levels of performance (Ibid.). Rolf is constantly unsure of which way he should go, because he is performing well musically at school, but is being attacked for it at home. He receives positive affirmations in public at school, and overwhelmingly negative ones at home. His striving to maintain internal consistency (Panksepp, 1990, 45) is torturous.

In spite of his difficulties, little Rolf presses on and has some hopeful moments in the midst of his painful junior high period. He has his first encounter with a student teacher at the junior high who is a trombone player himself, who offers him a free private lesson. The teacher, Mr. Goodman, actually has a high level of knowledge about the instrument and puts Rolf on a new mouthpiece, which improves his playing dramatically. But this also increases Rolf's conflict because, as his interest continues to grow and his success increases, his own family gets angrier and angrier.

The pattern is maintained throughout his first year of high school, where Rolf makes the top band in spite of all the opposition at home, which sometimes includes physical violence. At one point, his parents pull him completely out of band for an entire year, yet the band director manages to discreetly get him to play in the band without his parents' knowledge. All these accomplishments are well and good for Rolf, but the opposition from the family continues to increase, until finally in college, they prohibit Rolf from majoring in music, even though his band directors in high school encouraged him to go to Julliard on a music scholarship.

So, Rolf enters college as an accounting major, the only major his parents will allow him to take. He is very discouraged by this and finally after the first year, goes back to the trombone in spite of his parents' wishes and begins to take lessons with the trombone professor in the school's music department. He becomes the best student in the department, surpassing those who are music majors. The head of the trombone department, who is a world-famous soloist, offers to write a special Master's in Music program just for him so that he can make up deficiencies and be ready for a major symphony audition. Rolf is extremely excited about this concept and tells his family with predictable results. They blow up and violently eject him out of the house, with his father telling him that "he doesn't care who his teacher is, if you become a professional musician, you are no longer allowed in this house!" [2]

So now, Rolf has a major dilemma: will it be his parents' wishes or will it be music? This dilemma becomes the key on which all of his stage fright is based (Panksepp, 1990, 45). The deep-seated emotional conflict; the concept that playing music is against his parents' deepest wishes, will nag him his entire professional life. The stress of this conflict has taken a major toll on both his self-esteem and his emotional and physical well-being (Ibid., 47-48). At one point, Rolf begins to suffer from serious chronic illness due to the stress of this conflict with his parents (Ibid.). The conflict takes an emotional toll on him as well. (Ibid.). Because of this conflict, he is suffering from separation-distress, as explained by Panksepp in his article, in the

---

[2] Ibid.

Psychobiology of Stress, (Ibid., 46-47). In this work, he explains the separation distress/panic system in the brain, and its health consequences (Ibid.). He also explains the role of emotions in stress and brain chemistry (Ibid., 44-45). At this point, Rolf is experiencing these stressful emotions firsthand.

MEDICAL AND PSYCHOLOGICAL ANALYSIS

Upon examination by a physician, the diagnosis states that Rolf's body has been in chronic stress syndrome for years and that his hormonal balance is entirely upset, threatening his health. (Ibid., 44-47). The physician indicates that major lifestyle corrections in diet, exercise, sleep, etc., are necessary as well as physical therapy to put his body into order from years of abuse (Greene, *Performance Success*, 2002, 110-116). One important factor to note is that under extreme stress, the body will suffer and get out of balance due to overwork and overstimulation (Lee, 2002, 1, and Panksepp, 1990, 47-48).

All of these factors contribute to Rolf's chronic internal conflict. The more he tries to get beyond the painful circumstances of the stress caused by his parents' rejection of him and his musical career, the harder it becomes because of the physical and emotional breakdown caused by the stress which has become chronic. His energy level gets lower and lower, his emotions are a mess because of his massive internal conflict, and he has no spiritual resources most of the time, which would enable him to be inspired enough to make significant progress towards winning an audition (Ibid.).

At this stage, Rolf must either decide to give up music altogether, which would be a mistake, or face the painful reality of the consequences of his childhood and the massively negative impact it has had on his playing.

If he chooses to quit, this is too bad, having devoted a lifetime to music. If he decides to stay, he must begin to take stock of himself totally, honestly, and correct all these problems. In spite of all the stress and family opposition, Rolf chooses to go on.

STACY – VOCAL

Let us look at another example of a person struggling with stage fright issues, Stacy. Stacy is a singer of opera and orchestral works. She has been singing since she was 2. A gifted, phenomenally talented singer, she has sung in elementary school and high school. She received her first private instruction when she was sixteen while in high school.

MUSICAL CAREER

Singing has always come naturally and easily for Stacy. When she was finished with graduate school at one of the most prestigious singing schools in the world, she easily won the Metropolitan Opera contest for young artists.

In fact, Stacy has been a world-class singer since then, touring with many of the world's leading opera companies. She has performed at the most important venues in opera, La Scala in Milan, Covent Garden in London, and at the Metropolitan Opera in New York. Her guest performances have been with every major orchestra in the world, including the symphonies of Chicago, Berlin, New York, London, Vienna, and countless others. Stacy also has made numerous recordings on one of the world's premier classical labels, Deutsche Grammaphon. Stacy is a world-class star, ready to put her name in history along with the most famous sopranos of the century, Maria Callas, Joan Sutherland, and Beverly Sills, to name a few. But then something happens. Her voice fails; she begins to get throat problems that interfere with her singing and eventually cause her to stop altogether. What has happened?

Stacy had always gotten a little nervous before every performance, but nothing more than a few rushes of adrenaline prior to going on stage, part of the natural process of the body's mechanism for dealing with stressful situations successfully (Panksepp,1990, 45). Her voice was so natural, everything had come so easily, that she never had to really worry. She simply went out on stage each time, instantly overcame her jitters, and then sang beautifully, to overwhelming acclaim by audience and critics alike. Her overwhelming natural ability and her ability to summon it so easily was truly a rare occurrence.

The indications of Stacy's stage fright had been there all along, but the manifestations of it were very subtle. Since her performances had all come off so beautifully, and her career had continued to move on a rapidly upward ascent, she had ignored all the telltale warning signs that a serious problem was growing.

MEDICAL AND PSYCHOLOGICAL ANALYSIS

How did this happen? Why did a phenomenally gifted singer and performer with one of the most brilliant and naturally endowed voices in the world, see her career end too soon?

Let us look at Stacy's childhood. Stacy had come from a small town in Massachusetts. Both her parents were poor. Her father had worked at the local clothing factory all his life and had not finished high school. Her mother had finished high school but had had no further career aspirations outside of working as a clerk in a convenience store for six months until she married Stacy's father. Neither parent had any knowledge of music, other than a few songs they would hear on the radio. They treated their daughter's singing simply as an amusement and an annoyance, that would only be good for making her more charming to a potential husband. And hopefully, this husband would be a local man who also worked at the clothing factory or at a similar occupation.

There is a physiological connection to what we think and feel. (Panksepp, 1990, 44-47). The thoughts and emotions we possess and entertain are reflected by a certain chemical map in our neurons (Ibid.). The contents of the neurotransmitting chemicals, their proportional distribution, are directly related to whatever thought, emotion, or action we may undertake (Ibid.).As we begin to have more and more symptoms of stage fright, chemical changes are taking place in our body, in fact chemical and physiological imbalances are taking place in our body, and the body must then work to maintain balance, to maintain homeostasis (Ibid.,45). The longer these symptoms are ignored, the more these imbalances continue to wreak havoc on the body (Ibid., 44-47).

Every time Stacy had a symptom of stage fright, "nerves," and she ignored it, she set the stage for the condition to build up inside her to make her physiology related to singing become more and more unbalanced (Ibid.). Balance is a key ingredient of singing well. (Zouves, 1999, 7, 14). For example, the physiology of the area of the throat where the vocal cords lie (Fig. 4), is such that a certain amount of transported oxygen is necessary to feed the muscle cells of the muscles that surround and control the movement of the vocal cords to be able to sing well. If the oxygen supply to these muscles is reduced in any way, the muscles will begin to tense up, and not work as efficiently as they do when they are relaxed and have a full supply of oxygen (Frederiksen, 1996, 102). Every time a person has symptoms of stage fright, their body's tissues tense up in some way and they go into a stress reaction (Panksepp, 1990, 45).

One can analyze the contents of the neurotransmitting chemicals to see changes in their proportions when under stress (Fredrikson and Gunnarsson, 1992, 51). If the muscles surrounding the vocal cords continue to be oxygen starved, then the function of the vocal cords themselves will be impaired and any activity over the vocal cords will be strained and result in damage (Zouves, 1999, 14, and Frederiksen 1996, 102, 123). Although this process is subtle, over time if it continues, the vocal cords will become brittle and develop nodes and polyps and eventually break down as well (Jahn, M.D. 1999, 11, and Zouves, 1999, 14). Stacy's ignoring of the symptoms of stage fright caused her to increasingly abuse her vocal cords until they could no longer function, causing the final breakdown and loss of voice (Jahn, M.D. 1999, 11).

JIMMY – ORCHESTRAL

Let us know look at another case history, that of Jimmy. Jimmy, comes from a middle-class, very typical, suburban family. He is an only child. At the age of ten, he shows a particular interest in playing the French horn and so he begins to play the instrument in band. He goes along and is encouraged by his band director. He masters technical matters such as scales and arpeggios after a lot of

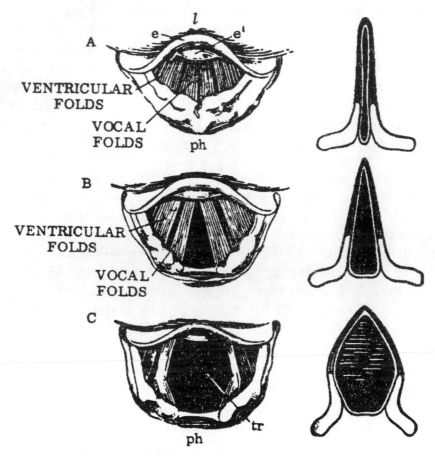

Fig. 33. The larynx as seen by means of the laryngo-
scope in different conditions of the glottis. A, while singing a high note; B, in quiet breathing; C, during a deep inspiration; l, base of tongue; e, upper free edge of epiglottis; e', cushion of epiglottis; ph, part of anterior wall of
pharynx; tr, trachea.

Fig. 4. Diagram of throat anatomy from Farkas (1962). Illustration originally from
the *Textbook of Anatomy and Physiology*, 13th edition, by Kimber, Gray, Stackpole,
and Leavell, published by The Macmillan Company, Ltd., 1955. Courtesy of
Teachers College, Columbia University, which now owns the copyright.

hard work. Jimmy enjoys music very much and his mother desperately wants him to have a career in music. As a child, she desired to have a career as a French horn player herself, but was prohibited by her father from doing so.

MUSICAL CAREER

Once in high school, Jimmy mother's gets him lessons with the most famous French horn teacher in the city from the Pittsburgh Symphony Orchestra. Jimmy's teacher encourages him, and works with him weekly. Jimmy works hard, and begins to make progress on some of the sophisticated concepts that his teacher gives him. He applies to, and then attends, one of the most famous musical schools in the country. At this school, he is good enough to get to be in the department, but is not considered the top player among his peers. He also takes lessons with a very flashy horn teacher, who is very big on technical performance, rather than artistic expression. This new horn teacher, unlike his previous teacher, knows nothing about artistic expression; he is only interested in note accuracy.

Those that are concerned only with not missing any notes, and not with artistic expression, are known as technical, or physical players. We will touch more on the physical player designation in more detail later. Adolph Herseth, the legendary first trumpet of the Chicago Symphony Orchestra, refers to these types of players as those who are "turning the crank" (Herseth, 1994-2000, 1:35) and not "telling a story" (Ibid.).

So Jimmy works hard, and makes very good progress as a technical player. When senior year comes around, and his fellow students are auditioning for jobs in major orchestras, Jimmy panics, and decides to go for a master's degree in performance instead (Panksepp, 1990, 46). His panic response is part of what Panksepp refers to as the "panic system" in the brain (Ibid.). He tells his mother that he is convinced he is not good enough to audition for a major orchestra right now and wants to choose his auditions carefully.

Now, Jimmy stays with his same technically orientated teacher through his master's degree program and when he is finished, he again considers his audition prospects. He decides that he is still not good enough for a major symphony audition, and so instead, decides to audition for one of the U.S. military bands in Washington, D.C., one of the nation's finest. He is very happy with this decision and is easily accepted. The band director has a markedly technical focus and so he is glad to have Jimmy in his band. Jimmy is glad to have a regular job in music, and is confident this will lead him to greater musical success in the future.

After enduring six weeks of the required military basic training, Jimmy goes to his first rehearsal. It is not what he has expected. The band director drives the band and pushes the players way beyond their physical limits. He is also under pressure from the commanding officer. The officer is not a musician, but as his superior, is free to make any commentary that he chooses about the music, and frequently does. Most of his commanding officer's comments have to do with note accuracy. The more wrong or missed notes the commanding officer hears, the more rehearsals he requires of the band, whether warranted or not (Parkland, 1994, 1).

As a result of this extra pressure from the commanding officer, Jimmy is forced to play far beyond what physically is possible. Because of this stress, Jimmy becomes obsessed with never missing a note under any circumstances, as this could result in a public reprimand from the band director, or even worse, an even more humiliating public reprimand from the commanding officer. In order to be able to play without missing a note under these stressful circumstances, Jimmy panics which causes poor judgement (Panksepp, 1990, 46).

Under the stress, his lip muscles, called the *embouchure* (italics mine) (Fig. 5) begin to lose muscle tone, making it harder and harder to produce a musical tone. To counteract this and to keep playing under his stressful circumstances, Jimmy presses harder and harder on his mouthpiece, which cuts off the blood supply to his lip muscles, making his playing increasingly less efficient (Frederiksen, 1996, 126). Thinking that more practice is the answer, he practices for a longer and longer duration outside of performance and rehearsal. This only stresses his lip muscles more (Ibid., 126).

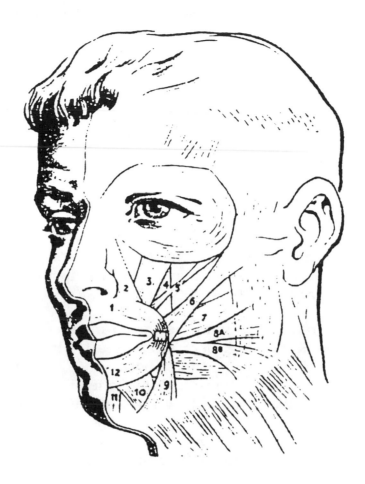

Fig. 9. M, modiolus. 1, orbicularis oris (upper lip portion). 2, levator labii sup. alaeque nasi. 3, levator labii superioris. 4, levator anguli oris. 5, zygomaticus minor. 6, zygomaticus major. 7, buccinator. 8a, risorius (masseteric strand). 8b, risorius (platysma strand). 9, depressor anguli oris. 10, depressor labii inferioris. 11, mentalis. 12, orbicularis oris (lower lip portion).

Fig 5. Embouchre musculature from Farkas (1962). Originally from the journal *Brass Today*, published by Besson and Company, Ltd., 1957, page 107, from the article "Problems of the Embouchure" written by Maurice Porter and edited by Frank Wright. © 1967 by Boosey & Hawkes Music Publishers Ltd. Reproduced by permission of Boosey & Hawkes Music Publishers Ltd.

MEDICAL AND PSYCHOLOGICAL ANALYSIS

Jimmy's famous teacher from high school, who had encouraged him to play in a fun, musical and efficient way, which used little or no pressure, and called for intelligent musical workload planning (Ibid., 158-159), was completely abandoned by Jimmy once he met his technical teacher in his undergraduate and graduate years. Now in this high-pressure situation, Jimmy is relying, on his college teacher's advice to get him through. His teacher's advice is to "get all the notes, that's the most important thing." The more Jimmy tries to "get all the notes," the more anxious he becomes. The more anxious he becomes, the more his body tenses up. The more his body tenses up, the harder it becomes to play. It is a losing battle of "push against shove" (Jacobs, 1994-1996, 1).

Because of this tension, Jimmy begins to miss more notes, without any idea why he is missing them. As a result, Jimmy's confidence is dangerously eroding over time both in his conscious and unconscious mind. His internal brain chemistry is also changing under such stress (Panksepp, 1990, 45). Now, Jimmy has entered into a situation where the only way he is able to play is from a purely physical and technical manner. This is what he has learned to do under the stress of the military band that he plays in.

After Jimmy's tour of duty with the military band ends, he gets a position as an Assistant Professor at Tannenbaum State University. As part of this position, he also automatically gets the position of Principal French Horn in the University Orchestra. Unfortunately, the level of playing at Tannenbaum State is not particularly high, so no one notices that Jimmy plays in such a tense style with such a tense sound. A tense sound indicates that the player is not in an artistic meditative state, and as a result, is not able to tell a musical story line (Greene, 2002, 1, and Frederiksen, 1996, 139). Jimmy teaches students, he practices on his own, and prepares himself, in his free time, for a possible major symphony audition.

Unfortunately, having no longer relied on his original teacher from the Pittsburgh Symphony, Jimmy practices from a purely technical and physical standpoint, rather than a musical one. Having learned this in his military band experience, Jimmy no longer knows any other way to play, and is still anxious about "getting all the right notes" whenever he plays, and he continues to operate always as if he is under a stressful situation (Panksepp, 1990, 45).

Finally, Jimmy's big moment comes and he receives word of a major symphony audition for a French horn position. Jimmy takes the audition, and wins due to a change in the musical outlook of the orchestra. Now Jimmy is a member of one of the world's best orchestras, but he is still convinced that he will never be quite good enough. So he works harder and harder, just like he did in the military band and just like his famous college teacher told him to, from a physical and technical level. His entire probationary period in the orchestra is extremely tense for him as he has no idea whether the orchestra will keep him or not. They do, due to further personnel changes among the decision makers. Now, Jimmy has finally made it in the orchestra, he has passed the probation period, he is a fully tenured member, and his job is secure. But doubts still linger; doubts still persist within him about his ability to play.

There is talk among the orchestra that Jimmy does not have the flexibility to blend with the other members of the orchestra. Some members say that his sound is not big enough; his sound is too tight and not particularly musical. Such talk fuels his self-doubt even further. Unfortunately, he practices even harder from a more technical and physical standpoint, which will only make the problem worse (Frederiksen, 1996, 126).

BOBBY – ORCHESTRAL

Bobby's case history is quite unique. He has never had any observable stage fright at all. Due to this unusual characteristic, I have nicknamed him "The Control," as he would be the perfect control subject for our study. Bobby grows up in a very musical family. His family is warm, caring and totally supportive of whatever he and his brothers may choose to do. The parents are both highly skilled amateur musicians. Not only is Bobby encouraged to play the clarinet, he is encouraged to play it at whatever level he wants, in front of mom and dad, grandparents, relatives, all at a supportive level that is age-appropriate. As he begins, he makes a few minor mistakes on his simple beginner's songs, which everyone overlooks because he is young and just starting. As he grows, the expectations get a little higher, but the quality of his teaching goes up as well, and naturally so does the level of his playing. This process goes on and continues on so that at every opportunity, Bobby is performing at the level or exceeding the level of play appropriate for his age group. Whatever stress he may encounter, he is oblivious to it, and his brain chemistry is totally geared to having fun with the instrument under all circumstances (Panksepp, 1990, 53).

His parents, his relatives, and his friends all warmly support his efforts on the clarinet and he enjoys the experience of playing, performing, and practicing immensely (Ibid.). He is always in a supportive environment while playing; he simply has not experienced any other way.

MUSICAL CAREER

Bobby wins band contests, solo contests, all the while having fun and enjoying the ease by which he can play. As he gets older, the contests become more competitive and intense, but Bobby never really notices and goes on to win them all. To him, these contests are just the gradual progression of the ability that he has always had along with all the fun and support that goes with it (Ibid.).

Time passes, he goes on to a prestigious music school, and is the top player in his department.

He continues to have even more fun in his budding musical career. He plays in the school's symphony orchestra, and is even asked to be a substitute in the major symphony that is in town. This big symphony is even more fun.

He plays as first clarinet in the local opera, and eventually gets asked to audition for the major symphony. He is not worried about this. Bobby simply sees this potential orchestra job as an opportunity to have more fun and, in this case, get paid nicely for it. It isn't much different than playing for his grandma when he was a child; it's just that now he is a little taller and can make his own money for a change. His brain chemistry is simply geared to associate playing music with fun, and with lots of emotional support, no matter what the circumstance (Ibid.).

MEDICAL AND PSYCHOLOGICAL ANALYSIS

Bobby is a very healthy individual and his parents and relatives have seen to it throughout his upbringing that he be well-nourished, get adequate sleep, and live a well-balanced social life in addition to his musical activities (Panksepp, 1990, 47). Because of this constant support and care, and because of the gradual and very supportive approach to public performance provided by his family, his body is always completed relaxed whenever he performs, for that matter, whenever he picks up his instrument to play.

Since as we have discussed above and previously, Bobby sees musical performance as a fun and approved activity, he never feels any stress. So he is always in the optimum psychological state for the highest level of performance (Ibid.). Being in this state also is the most efficient way to get the best musical results with the least effort, although of course, some effort is still required. Music for Bobby is a joy.

3

TRADITIONAL SOLUTIONS

BACKGROUND

Stage fright, or performance anxiety, is one of the most devastating experiences a performer can ever have. The condition is characterized by varying degrees of insecurity and doubt (Greene, *Fight Your Fear*, 2001, 72-73). These doubts and insecurities make one question who he or she is, or what kind of abilities one may have (Ibid.). All memory of any ability is erased through a numbing process – the performer feels thrown back to an entirely elementary level.

Previously, we have discussed some of the physiological aspects of stage fright in Chapter 1. There are a few more additional physiological characteristics of stage fright that can be readily observed by the person while they are suffering from the condition. Stage fright puts the performer in a stress reaction, which causes the body to become less efficient. Cortisone levels are increased (Fredrikson and Gunnarsson, 1992, 52), blood pressure and pulse are elevated (Ibid.), the mucous membranes, in particular those in the mouth, are dry, thinking and vision become more narrow and singularly focused (Gladwell, 2000, 88). This is exactly the opposite of what is needed for a successful and meaningful performance (Ibid., 85) and certainly the opposite of what would be needed for playing at the highest levels (Frederiksen, 1996, 159).

PHARMACEUTICAL – INDERAL®

The prescription drug, propranolol hydrochloride, which goes by the trade name, INDERAL®, is the most commonly used drug by classical musicians to counteract the symptoms associated with stage fright. It is taken sometime prior to the audition, the specific time period determined by the administering physician based on the individual (Goodman and Gilman, 2001, 253, and Medical Economics, Co., Inc., 2002, 3515). It is most often taken orally and so is conveniently administered (Goodman and Gilman, 2001, 253-254). Since it is in tablet form, it is easy for musicians to take their dosage sometime prior to their audition at the audition site itself. It is normally used to treat a variety of conditions, including hypertension, angina, and intravenously for life-threatening arrhythmia, but has been prescribed by physicians for stage fright for some time (Ibid., 254).

Although INDERAL® is generally known among classical musicians to calm nerves (Lanier, 2002, 1), the artistic and musical results it engenders are poor (Scarlett, 2002, 1). We will speak more of this later in Chapter 6.

FREDRIKSON AND GUNNARSSON'S STUDY

COMPARISON OF HIGH AND LOW-ANXIOUS GROUPS

A marvelous study was done in 1992 by the Swedish researchers Mats Fredrikson and Robert Gunnarsson. In this study, musicians were studied for the effects of stage fright in public performance. The neuroendocrine, cardiovascular, and what the researchers refer to as subjective reactions, were studied. The subjective reaction component refers to the analysis of the quality of musical performance as graded by two members of the Musical Academy in Stockholm. The neuroendocrine chemicals that were studied for activation level were, epinephrine, norepinephrine hormones of the adrenal medulla, and cortisol, which are secreted by the adrenal cortex as mentioned earlier (Fredrikson and Gunnarsson, 1992, 52). The subjects were divided into two groups in order to analyze their stage fright reactions in performance: the high-anxious and the low-anxious (Ibid., 53). The cardiovascular parameter studied was heart rate (HR) (Ibid., 52).

The high-anxious group was characterized by having experienced some muscle tremor previously during public performance due to stage fright (Ibid., 53). This factor was used to differentiate them from the low-anxious group who never had such tremor during public performance (Ibid., 53). All subjects had no known skill impairment (Ibid., 54). The subjects played before a music faculty member for evaluation of their playing.

Another faculty member listened to tapes of their performance, but was not present at the performance (Ibid., 55). The professor who evaluated the tapes was blind to whether the performers were in the high or the low-anxious group (Ibid.). The musicians were also analyzed for neuorendocrine and cardiovascular activity during a separate private performance, but did not having their playing analyzed subjectively for artistic quality.

Fredrikson and Gunnarsson note through Analysis of Variance of the data in Table 1, that excretion of epinephrine and cortisol are significantly increased during public performances for both groups compared to private performances. Norepinephrine excretion, for private to public performance decreased for the high-anxious group and increased for the low-anxious group (Table 1). The heart rates (HR) increased for both groups from private to public performance, although the high-anxious group (HR) increased more in each case (Fig. 6).

For the quality of performance ratings, which Fredrikson and Gunnarsson refer to as the subjective score, the quality rating given for the high-anxious group is lower than the low-anxious group when the public performance is analyzed by a professor attending the performance. As mentioned above, a tape is made of this performance (Ibid., 58). When the taped performance is analyzed anonymously by another professor, he gives the low-anxious group a lower quality score than the high-anxious group. He also gives the high-anxious group exactly the same score as the professor attending the concert did (Ibid., Fig. 7). These results mean that the quality rating scores of the low-anxious group went down from the live evaluation to a taped one (Ibid., Fig. 7).

Table 1

Epinephrine, norepinephrine and cortisol excretion expressed in pmol/min during private and public performance in high- and low-anxious string musicians

| | High-anxious | | Low-anxious | |
	Private	Public	Private	Public
Epinephrine	41.9	60.1	47.8	104.6
Norepinephrine	181.7	178.7	139.0	162.7
Cortisol	267.4	359.1	242.7	311.4

Table 1. Epinephrine, norepinephrine and coritsol excretion from Fredrikson and Gunnarsson (1992). Reprinted from *Biological Psychology* 33, Fredrikson, Mats and Robert Gunnarsson, "Psychobiology of stage fright. The effect of public performance on neuroendocrine, cardiovascular, and subjective reactions," page 56, © 1992 with permission from Elsevier Science.

M. Fredrikson and R. Gunnarsson / Psychobiology of stage fright

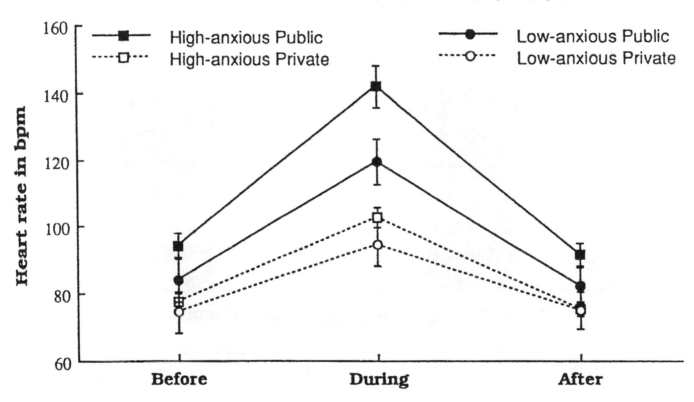

Fig. 2. HR before, during and after private and public performance in high- and low-anxious string musicians. Vertical bars denote the standard error of the mean.

Fig. 6.   Heart Rate graph from Fredrikson and Gunnarson (1992). Reprinted from *Biological Psychology* 33, Fredrikson, Mats and Robert Gunnarsson, "Psychobiology of stage fright: The effect of public performance on neuroendocrine, cardiovascular, and subjective reactions," page 57, © 1992 with permission from Elsevier Science.

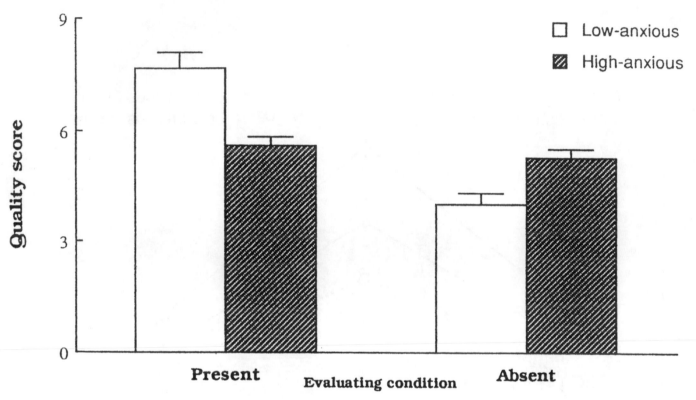

Fig. 3. Ratings of musical quality during public performance in high- and low-anxious string musicians by an attending professor (present) and done blindly from recording by a professor who had not been present (absent). Vertical bars denote the standard error of the mean.

Fig. 7. Ratings of musical quality table from Fredrikson and Gunnarsson (1992). Reprinted from *Biological Psychology* 33, Fredrikson, Mats and Robert Gunnarsson, "Psychobiology of stage fright: The effect of public performance on neuroendocrine, cardiovascular, and subjective reactions," page 58, © 1992 with permission from Elsevier Science.

Fredrikson and Gunnarsson's conclusion of this study was that the quality of musical performance, (subjective factor), the heart rate, and the neuroendocrine factors (excretion of NE, EP, and cortisol) associated with stage fright "were poorly" related (Ibid., 60).

REINTERPRETATION OF INITIAL RESULTS BASED ON PROFESSIONAL PERFORMANCE EXPERIENCE

My suggestion as a professional musician who has played with members of the Chicago Symphony Orchestra,[1] and who has had much experience with auditions and many performances at a high level, is that these two Swedish researchers' conclusions are in error. First of all, the faster heart rate (HR), for the high-anxious group, makes sense from a performer's experience. From my personal observation as a professional musician, if you have a greater degree of stage fright, and have muscle tremor, you are in the high-anxious group defined by the Swedish researchers' criteria. I have had such tremor in the past, and I can affirm that in the high-anxious state, your heart rate is certainly far greater than when you are going through less stressful experiences.

But I respectfully disagree with the researchers' analysis that the quality of musical performance, (the subjective factor), the heart rate (physiological factor), and the neuroendocrine factors (excretion of NE, EP, and cortisol) associated with stage fright "were poorly" related (Ibid., 60).

The fact that the heart rate increased with both groups when comparing private performances with public performances and that the high-anxious group had higher (HR) in both cases is consistent with my many hundreds of experiences as a professional musician and the observations I have made of many of my colleagues as well as the discussions I have had with them regarding performance and stage fright. What is not consistent with my performing experience and observation of performers in many actual audition and public

---

[1] I am a member and perform with the Ravinia Festival Orchestra, the majority of whose members for the classical programs that I play on, are from the Chicago Symphony Orchestra.

performance situations, is the researchers' lack of a real reason or stated relationship related to the differences in neuroendocrine levels observed between the high-anxious and the low-anxious group (Ibid., 60).

I believe that the high-anxious group truly suffers from severe stage fright based on my experience and observation as a professional musician.   I believe that the low-anxious group does not suffer from stage fright at all, but is simply "keyed up" for the act of performing (Greene, 2002, 98-99).   Don Greene, PhD, of the faculty of the Julliard School, and the world's leading authority on stage fright management, insists that "centering up" is crucial for performance success (Ibid.).   You must get the biochemistry activated to perform well.   However, you cannot get too "up," otherwise you move into a severe stage fright reaction and must "center down" in order to rebalance your physiology to play well (Ibid., 56-57).

Looking also at the studies of Panksepp (1990), he makes a great case for the idea that there may be additional neurochemicals that cancel out the effect of those neurochemicals produced under stress so that the person can perform well under stress (Panksepp, 1990, 46). Although he states that this is a new frontier in science, he gives examples of why this may be true and should be studied further (Ibid.).   Panksepp (1990) believes that these positive mitigating neurochemicals are related to the joyful, but not well-known effect of play (Ibid.). And this is *exactly* what I think explains the difference between the levels of neuroendocrine compounds between the two groups in Fredrikson and Gunnarsson's 1992 study.   When a musician is performing well, they are truly at play, like a child (Jacobs, 1995, p. 1).   The "up" low-anxious group is at play when they perform.   And so, according to Panksepp (1990), there must be as stated above some chemical changes that occur in the neuroendocrine system while at play for the "up" group (Panksepp, 1990, 45, 51).

So in the Fredrikson and Gunnarsson study, the much more dramatic increase in epinephrine excretion in the low-anxious "up" group, occurred because they were positively "up" for the performance and played well. This was shown by the fact that the live music professor who rated them gave them a much higher quality score than he did for the high-anxious group (Fig 5).   It is worthy of note that epinephrine excretion was greater in the low-anxious than the high-anxious group during public performance. This suggests that our low-anxious group has a greater degree of adrenal medullary activation during public performance which is consistent with my contention, that low-anxious performers are "up" to a greater extent than performers in the high-anxious group during public performance. The lack of significant changes in norepinephrine, or cortisol excretion in public performance compared to private performance, regardless of high-anxious or low-anxious group, suggests that these neurochemical indices are poorer neurochemical markers of stage fright. This could be a similar effect to what Panksepp (1990) states in the mitigating functions of oxytocin and vasopressin (sic) under stress (Ibid.).

It was Fredrikson and Gunnarsson's observations that the second professor who listened to the tapes in private, came up with the same score for the high-anxious group as the professor who evaluated the high-anxious group live. This same anonymous professor who evaluated the tapes also came up with a worse score for the low-anxious "up" group (Ibid., 60). Fredrikson and Gunnarsson stated that the "pattern of results" "does not seem to relate to performance quality or subjective reactions during acutal performance." (Ibid.). I think the researchers misinterpreted these results. It is my contention that the two Swedish researchers know nothing about the unreliability of listening to taped performances and the near impossibility of getting an accurate evaluation. Even the Chicago Symphony Orchestra, when requesting tapes for auditionees who live far away, publish a warning about the unreliability of analyzing any kind of taped performance (see appendix). The unreliability of taped performance evaluations is something that Fredrikson and Gunnarsson would not be aware of, not being professional musicians, so their conclusions regarding what they consider subjective evaluations are in error.

Therefore, I hold that the results of their experiments are consistent and make sense for performers who are "up" for the performance and play well, the low-anxious group. They do not, however, make sense for the performers who suffer from severe stage fright and do not play well, the high-anxious group.

MOVING FROM HIGH TO LOW-ANXIOUS GROUP

Those in the high-anxious group as defined by Fredrikson and Gunnarsson face a dilemma. They may love music but are crippled by the weight of their stage fright, and cannot perform well at all.

Traditional advice in the classical music field is unhelpful for those in the high-anxious group who want to continue performing.

Many times their teacher's advice to avoid stage fright is to "prepare carefully" or "(j)ust relax" (Greene, 2002, 1). But for those who are in the high-anxious group (Fredrikson and Gunnarsson, 1992, 53) of stage fright, this is not enough. The advice to prepare carefully always falls on deaf ears – for at some point as soon as there is a deadline, the performer falls apart and cannot even prepare because he or she has stage fright even in the preparation phase! So their preparation becomes a shambles. This is particularly true of performers who came from a family background with a history of psychological or other abuse.

In cases where parental support is lacking AND outright opposition to a student's musical career occur, the student is faced with some difficult choices (Caruso and Tetrazzini, 1975, 40-41). The student must have the best teacher available and must immediately begin working on those personal issues that severely impair their ability to perform (Greene, 2002, 1). A student can practice and practice in a proper and efficient way, but still may be unable to perform in public and at auditions at their best level due to prior mental blockages (Ibid., 2).

As we have seen from Fredrikson and Gunnarsson's study, at the severest levels in the high-anxious group, these disorders can have a very strong physical (muscle tremor) and chemical component (neuroendocrine), resulting in increased levels of cortisone production and release by the adrenal cortex as well as depletion of adrenaline, from the adrenal medulla (Hoffmann, 2000, vol. 3). This is the result of the student always being in an "overdrive" situation, that is, always in a stress state, which has been commonly known as the "fight-or-flight" response (Hoffmann, 2000, vol. 3).

In this stressed state, the heart rate is increased, breathing is shallow and at a faster rate than normal (Greene, *Fight Your Fear*, 2001, 46-49), and mental functioning is impaired (Ibid., 72-73). The student cannot think clearly, and is in no way relaxed, because the muscles of the body are unnaturally tense. In very severe cases, the body shuts down in the same way as the prey of a predator would prior to being killed and eaten. There is recently on record, the experience of a medical professional who was in the process of being eaten by a shark after having been attacked. Amazingly, she was able to describe the experience (*Chicago Sun-Times*, 31 August 2001).

In severe cases of stage fright, the student may be in a state of sheer terror.[2]

In the next chapter, we are going to look at some ways in which members of the high-anxious group with stage fright, can move to the low-anxious "up" group that is "keyed up" for performance and play well (Fredrikson and Gunnarsson 1992, 53, and Greene, 2002, 98-99).

---

[2] This is my personal observation as a professional musician.

4

NEW SOLUTIONS TO STAGE FRIGHT

HISTORY

The majority of teaching methods for stage fright in instrumental music involve the repetitive instruction in the mechanical functions of the instrument, much like the teaching of multiplication tables to children in the lower grades. These mechanical tables help the beginning student gain familiarity with the hand-eye motor coordination skills necessary to produce an adequate sound for the first time and serve as a means for the student to be able to re-create that sound in the future. The theory here is that constant perfect repetition over time will increase the confidence to such a level that they will never make a mistake under even the most stressful of situations.

Just as multiplication tables serve as building blocks to the eventual mastery of algebra, trigonometry, calculus, and beyond, a beginning musician must also learn fundamentals. The building blocks for the young musician are the diatonic major and minor scales, the twelve-tone chromatic scale, the basics of rhythm and harmony, and if they are taught well, the beginnings of sight-singing, known as solfeggio.

In the case of the brass instruments, the beginner must be taught how to hold the instrument properly, how to breathe in order to produce sound, and have at least minimal instruction in how to place one's lips on the mouthpiece in order to produce a sound. Once these basic physical skills are mastered, the student is typically encouraged to play major, minor, and chromatic scales over and over and also to play simple melodies for rhythmic training. Such melodies serve to develop the young student's ear for a quality musical sound.

Throughout the typical training period of a young musician, from grade school through the college years, the basic skills mentioned above are continually developed at an ever-increasing level of complexity. Once the student has reached a certain level of mastery, they are prepared to go on to higher levels of musical study. At some point, the student is required to cease becoming a student and become a musical artist, a musician. (Frederiksen, 1996, 94).

The transition from student to artist is a gradual process, and one gets the feeling at first that they are starting over from the beginning. In a sense, they are. Because once a sufficient command of the instrument has been achieved through the technical mastery of the basic skills, the student must then discard any conscious thought in the performance of the fundamentals learned from the beginning. That is, these fundamentals must have become so automatic that the mind is totally focused on the emotional message and story line of the music itself. In orchestral music, there is not always a clear story line, but there is definitely an emotional component. The advanced performer must decide what kind of story line or emotion must be expressed (Copland, 1953, 13-18).

In order to be able to make the leap from a strictly mechanical performance to the larger experience of expressing the true language of orchestral music, one must be able to connect the notes not as random markings on a page, but as a series of continuously flowing ideas, or musical sentences, that tell the story. These musical sentences are called phrases (Scholes, 1952, 455). A series of such sentences form a musical paragraph, and each movement in a musical composition is composed of paragraphs that constitute a chapter in the musical story, the piece.

Such an esoteric transition can only be made through use of the unconscious (Greene, *Fight Your Fear*, 2001, 51). If a student continues to focus on the mechanics of playing, and not the message they are trying to convey, the result will be a boring, mechanical performance (Frederiksen, 1996, 94). In order to achieve a truly musical performance, conscious messages from prior training must be ignored, and practice must now focus on thinking only of the musical story line and its message and putting this into the imagination. The artist must now make musical statements, and no longer ask questions while playing (Frederiksen, 1996, 158).

Now this process is not as simple as it may appear. The mind must be strictly disciplined in order to ignore any and all superfluous messages so that the unconscious can operate freely (Greene, *Fight Your Fear*, 56). To quote the first trumpet player of the Chicago

Symphony, the legendary Adolph Herseth, "Playing has less to do with the mouth than the ear...(y)ou have to start with a precise sense of how something should sound. Then, instinctively, you modify your lip and your breathing and the pressure of the horn to obtain that sound." (Doherty, 1994, 102). Playing is not primarily a physical process. At the highest level, it is a process solely driven by the unconscious (Frederiksen, 1996, 137).

To make such a psychological leap that one completely trusts one's ability on the instrument and plays solely from the unconscious is akin to diving off the high dive into a pool. At first this can be a rather frightening experience. But as time goes on, it is something that becomes quite thrilling as the routine switch into the unconscious is something the performer becomes accustomed to doing. In the words of Adolph Herseth himself, "Man alive, what a kick this is!" (Neidig, 1977, 38). To be in this trusting state is also a spiritual experience that enables the musical artist to transcend from the ordinary into the extraordinary. When an artist can do this, they take the audience to the highest level of experience, which results in a memorable performance. Such a performance is more than just "getting all the right notes" (Herseth, 1999, 3).

In order to achieve such a state, the performer must disregard any negative prior training, assumptions, and anxiety about what is to come up. He or she must simply focus on the music in a childlike manner, with total trust, sincerity, and lack of worry (Greene, *Fight Your Fear*, 2001, 57). At the same time he or she is acting as an adult paying complete attention to conveying a musical message within the framework of the music itself. The great musical artists have always had such ability. Unfortunately, many performers cannot make the leap between technical mastery and the highest levels of musical expression and artistry. Many do not realize that they must go back to a childlike state in order to achieve such mastery and that there is where the answer lies, not in more and more hours of repeated, frustrating and pointless practice (Frederiksen, 1996, 93-95).

Achieving such a childlike state and being able to summon it at will takes much practice (Gallwey, n.d.). At the higher levels of playing, the mental factors are of more concern than the physical (Frederiksen, 1996, 93). At the highest level, spiritual factors are predominant and essential to creating consistency in the performer (Gallwey, n.d.). The performer must feel safe. Any physical problems in playing can be corrected through the redirection and unblocking of one's mind to allow the unconscious to work freely in the musical realm (Ibid. and Greene, 2002, 2).

It is interesting to note that those who have started from an early age performing with strong emotional encouragement from their parents tend to suffer less from the stage fright phenomenon as they progress in their artistic careers (Frederiksen, 1996, 93, and Lavatelli, 1970, 5)[1].   This is because those individuals, through the example and encouragement provided by their parents, began with the simple belief that not only was performing encouraged, but it was fun and approved activity.   As the years went on, the growing performer retained such an attitude in his emotional memory.   The result was that even as music matters became more and more complex, the performer rarely suffered from stage fright (Neidig, 1977, 38) regardless of the pressures involved (Doherty, 1994, 100).   Our case history above of Bobby, from chapter two, is a classic example of such a situation.

AUTO-TRANSMISSION OF NEUROTRANSMITTERS

DISCUSSION

I believe that a musician like Bobby, from our case history, is able to deal with the stress of performing by consciously altering his neurochemistry, in a manner similar to that suggested by Panksepp (1990, 45) regarding the release of neurochemicals that are automatically able to counteract the effect of the neurochemicals normally released under stress (Ibid.).   Panksepp suggests that these mitigating chemicals are somehow released because of the effects of play (Ibid.).

---

[1] This is consistent with Piaget's interactional point of view that as mental structures develop from an early age, the effect is cumulative. From Lavatelli (1970) as indicated.   See the reference shown for further elaboration of this idea.

CASE STUDIES - HERSETH, SCARLETT, AND JACOBS

Play is exactly how the three greatest brass players from the Chicago Symphony Orchestra, the legendary Adolph Herseth, William Scarlett, trumpets, and the late Arnold Jacobs, tuba, (Fig. 8) consistently describe their attitude when they perform. They are always *playing, like a child* (Italics mine) (Jacobs, 1994-1996). They are always consistent, and are joyful about what they do because for them it is child's play (Ibid., and Scarlett 2002, and Neidig, 1977, 41). What I am suggesting is that these three great men, through the effects of play as described by Panksepp (1990, 45), must auto-transmit, send signals within their brain and the autonomic nervous system to produce the appropriate neurochemistry to mitigate any negative effects of the stress of performance, just like children must do when they play (Panksepp, 1990, 45).

TRANSITION FROM HIGH TO LOW-ANXIOUS GROUP

DISCUSSION AND OBSERVATION

Unfortunately, those aspiring performers who did not have the support and security of a positive background often suffer from stage fright and its related lack of confidence. They also may not have the necessary "nerves of steel" needed for advancement to the top of the profession. For them, it is my personal experience that intense analysis into the emotional causes and sources of psychological blockages that cause stage fright must be undertaken.

From the observation of both myself and many other professional musicians in all manner of performance and practice situations, these emotional blockages are the source of the stage fright of the members of Fredrikson and Gunnarsson's high-anxious group (Fredrikson and Gunnarsson, 1992, 53). Another way to express this is, *the inability to perform up to one's level when confronted with the performance situation* (italics mine, Greene, *Fight Your Fear*, 2001, p.72-73). It should be encouraging to note that all such stage fright situations are directly related to prior emotional and psychological factors, which can be investigated and resolved in order to eliminate their unnecessary interference in performance.

THERAPIES NEEDED TO MAKE TRANSITION

It is my opinion, based on my own experience and observation, that musical study alone does not guarantee that the student will solve their problems, eliminate stage fright and become a world-class performer. The student needs to be disciplined and thorough in order to reach the level of their teachers who are already preeminent in their field. At this stage of development, much depends on the student's willingness to put in time and effort on, not only their deficiencies in playing their instrument, but also to spend time discovering and solving the personal blockages (Smith, n.d.) resulting from any inconsistent support for their musical career from parents during the childhood years.

The amount of time spent in such personal study depends on the individual's aptitude for such research, personal creativity, ingenuity and the severity of the deprivation of emotional support from the family during childhood years. If the situation was not too severe, then certain problems of stage fright will be solved and corrected by a minimal amount of study and personal investigation and by increasing the amount of public performance in less stressful situations (Greene, 2002, xiv). These practice performances may be used as a laboratory situation (Ibid., 112-113).

As the severity of support deprivation increases, the student involved will have to spend considerably more time on personal study to correct the problems at hand (Cameron, 1992, 11-13). In those extreme cases where the student was seriously deprived of parental support in childhood, perhaps even facing violent opposition to a musical career, intense study may be needed over a period of years. There are many traditional and alternative therapies available today that will help the student from such an abusive background to rise up to a position of positive balance. Some examples, are psychological counseling, support groups, and physically orientated therapies. Some examples of physically orientated therapies, are Tai Chi, Reiki, Yoga, and Rolfing.

Diet and general health matters can also be examined, and any serious health problems can be discussed with a physician. The point is, the student should do whatever is necessary, as long as it is not harmful, to get themselves back in balance from their childhood trauma, so that they can become a fully functional adult and pursue their career with unlimited and positive success. Once at a position of positive emotional balance, they can make rapid progress and move on to success in their careers.

CASE STUDY – CARUSO

If the student from an extreme situation is willing to make such an intense commitment and put in the time necessary to research and correct such emotional blockages, the rewards are great indeed and will result in a promising musical career. The famous tenor, Enrico Caruso, is a perfect example of a musical artist who came from an extreme situation. At the age of fifteen, when the young Caruso declared to his father that he wished to pursue a career in music, he was thrown out of the house, never to return (Caruso and Tetrazzini, 1975, 40-41).

Fortunately, for Caruso, he received ever-increasing encouragement from teachers and others outside his family along the way (Ibid., 40-44). This is a classic example of the value of the individual working their individual problems out so that they can fully pursue a performing career at the highest levels. Caruso was a tremendous student of himself and his craft (Ibid., 45-71). As a result of his diligence, the world enjoyed one of the greatest voices of the twentieth century.

In the next chapter, we will see that Rolf, one of our case studies, has made significant progress in moving from the high-anxious group to the low-anxious group (Fredrikson and Gunnarsson, 1992, 53).

Figure 8a. *Left to right.* Adolph "Bud" Herseth, and the author in front of Orchestra Hall, Chicago, January, 1997. Used with permission of Adolph Herseth. Photo ©1999 by Wendy Goode.

Figure 8b. *Left to right.* The author, and William Scarlett, at Mr. Scarlett's Studio in northern Illinois, April, 2001. Used with permission of William Scarlett. Photo ©2001 by Wendy Goode.

Figure 8c. *Left to right.* The author, and Arnold Jacobs at Mr. Jacobs' studio in Chicago, January, 1996. Used with permission of Dallas Jacobs. Photo ©1996 by Wendy Goode.

Figure 8d. *Left to right.* The author, and Wendy Goode, after a performance of Leonard Bernstein's *Candide* with the Bismarck-Mandan Symphony, January, 2003. Photo ©2003 by Wendy Goode.

5

REMARKS ON CASE HISTORIES

REVISITING THE FIRST FOUR

ROLF

In the case of Rolf, he was always in a severe stress reaction. Not having the emotional support of his family, but instead encountering open hostility from his parents and brother to his musical career and interests as a young boy, put him in an unsafe situation psychologically and emotionally. That situation him caused the corresponding physiological stress reaction of "fight-or-flight" and "separation distress" (Panksepp, 1990, 45). His body had never really been conditioned for any other state in his relationship with music, other than this stress reaction, because his family had consistently attacked him every time he played, enjoyed, talked about, or had anything to do with music.

Unlike Bobby, for Rolf, music was never associated with joy, pleasure, or any kind of positive experience. Instead, music was simply associated with pain, struggle, and a fight for his life, which always translated itself into the primitive physiological response of "fight-or-flight" and the sadness and stress of "separation distress" (Panksepp, 1990, 45). In fact, even practicing on his own, and certainly in preparation for any performance, Rolf suffered from stage fright and all its symptoms. The remarkable thing in Rolf's case is that he continued to play. What Rolf did develop in response to such negative unconscious programming through the reactions of his parents and family, was a very powerful deep-seated belief that he needed to persist with music until the time he would be in a safer, less stressful situation. This could be a survival strategy similar to what Panksepp (1990, 51), proposes for those with separation distress.

At the present time, Rolf has persisted in his musical career, and has spent a number of years exploring and examining the negative programming from his family on all levels, and has consulted with a wide range of medical professionals. He has been able to determine not only what his problems are, but through extensive research and personal development, has come up with successful ways to deal with his stage fright. At the current time, he is working not only with his famous teacher from the Pittsburgh Symphony, but is also working with a nationally famous stage fright and audition coach. Rolf will be auditioning for the Pittsburgh Symphony in a number of weeks, and he plans to win the 2nd trombone position there. His situation is a success story.

STACY

Stacy has not fared so well. Because she was never consciously aware of the negative programming from her childhood and chose to completely ignore it, she has been totally devastated and unable to recover from the devastating loss of her phenomenal voice. At this point, she must go back and examine all aspects of her life that have been impacted by her career devastation and be brutally honest about the sources of those negative consequences. She must examine all medical aspects of her condition. She must also examine and seek expertise to repair the extensive emotional damage with a strong focus on her childhood experiences. It is unclear whether she will ever regain her voice.

JIMMY

Eventually over time, Jimmy finds that his lips begin to give out, and within a few years, the tissues of his lip, and their surrounding muscles, his *embouchure* (Fig. 5), can no longer cope with the stress, and he becomes barely able to play. As a result of the pressure and stress, he sustains nerve damage in the tissues and muscles of his lips.

Unfortunately for Jimmy, he became unable to conquer his stress-related psychological tension in his horn playing. He had a growing dystonia in all the muscles related to playing which eventually caused him to lose full control of his lip musculature. The result is that he misses notes constantly and his sound is uneven and poor. But worst of all, he has no way, from his technical standpoint, to correct this problem.

What has happened here is that Jimmy's stage fright, as manifested by his self-doubt, reinforced by a military band system and a college teacher who operates in a crisis management teaching style, has taken over and caused the physiology that plays the French horn to shut down. He is forced to leave the orchestra. He never realized that this was happening until it was too late.

BOBBY

Bobby becomes a world-famous clarinet player in the world's most famous orchestra, and has a wonderful and long career. He feels truly satisfied.

6

CONCLUSION

RETURNING TO THE ISSUE

Severe stage fright in the high-anxious group (Fredrikson and Gunnarsson, 1992, 45) causes the heart rate to increase, muscle tremor, confused and panic thinking, profuse sweating, edema, and other less common reactions (Greene, *Fight Your Fear*, 2001, 46-49). All these actions interfere with an effective musical performance. If the performer with severe stage fright tries to follow traditional advice of simply more practice and performance, it becomes a hopeless situation. The more the performer with stage fright performs and in severe cases even practices, the worse the stage fright gets.

INDERAL® AND THE CLASSICAL MUSIC INDUSTRY

Some performers try to take what seems like a simple solution to the remediating methods described in Chapter 4 above by dosing themselves with pharmaceuticals, with the most popular being the prescription drug, INDERAL®.

The use of INDERAL®, a beta-adrenergic antagonist, generically known as propranolol hydrochloride (Goodman and Gilman, 2001, 253), is common among classical musicians for use in auditions. This drug is known as a non-specific beta blocker, blocking both $\beta1$ and $\beta2$ receptors (Ibid.). One of INDERAL®'s therapeutic uses is to treat hypertension (Ibid., 252). The drug lowers the heart rate (HR) and blood pressure (Ibid., 253), and evens out the performer's hyper-excited stress state to a more even level (Lanier, 2002, 1).

The musical interpretative difficulty that arises is that such a performance becomes a boring and mechanical one. (Scarlett, 2002, 1). The exciting element that gives the music a unique inspiration is eliminated.   In the words of William Scarlett of the Chicago Symphony Orchestra, this results in a "placid, colorless" performance with "very little emotion" and there is nothing for the audience (Ibid.). The intimate subtlety and excitement within musical phrasing is evened out.   The performance becomes bland, and uninteresting (Ibid.).   Experiments that attempt to electronically mimic human emotive expression in music have resulted in a similar mechanical effect (Clynes, 1982, 372).

At the highest levels of performance, this pharmaceutical approach is ineffective because the high degree of subtlety required in order to express oneself musically becomes lost. This subtlety gets obliterated by the tranquilizing effect of such drugs (Medical Economics Co., Inc. 2002, 3515) and the musical story line becomes lost. Music devoid of human emotion becomes lifeless (Scarlett, 2002, 1, and Walter, 1994).

PHYSICAL PLAYING - A COUNTERFEIT SOLUTION TO AUTO-TRANSMISSION

Many people who play brass instruments, in particular, fall into the trap of highly technical playing that is not driven by delivering an artistic message, a musical story line (Frederiksen, 1996, 152). Jimmy, our case study from Chapters 2 and 5, is what is known as a "physical player" (Scarlett, 2002, p.1). Many times, these individuals can pass auditions and advance fairly far in the profession due to oversights on the part of the audition committees making the decision, but the orchestra, the audience, and the physical players themselves always suffer in the end. Physical playing will never substitute for the kind of magnificent artistic playing that comes from auto-transmission as we discussed in Chapter 4 in the cases of Herseth, Scarlett, and Jacobs, all of the Chicago Symphony Orchestra.

FULL TRANSITION FROM HIGH TO LOW-ANXIOUS GROUP

Successful performance of music in an audition or concert, requires that the student be totally relaxed and in a Zen-like state of mind in order to be at the optimal performance level (Gallwey, 1974, 31). This is exactly the opposite of what occurs when a person is in the severely stressed state described above of those in the high-anxious group. The musical results that come from such a severely stressed state are disastrous. The performance will mostly likely be a total failure, an experience that will further erode the distressed student's fragile level of confidence.

As it has been written in Chapters 4 and 5, this level of failure can be corrected and redirected into success through the examination and reworking of all the physical, emotional, psychological, and spiritual difficulties that the student has which result in failure at the moment of performance (Greene, *Fight Your Fear*, 2001, 6-7). Once these difficulties are identified, understood, and corrected, then it is a much easier matter to train the student in effective performance techniques so that they may catch up and surpass their peers. They can then join the low-anxious group (Fredrikson and Gunnarsson, 1992, 53). The reason I am suggesting that these students will most likely surpass their peers is because once the process of intense self-examination is undertaken and successfully accomplished, the student will be much better in tune with what makes them work internally than others, and this will give them a decisive advantage in their ability to learn and play brilliantly (Greene, *Audition Success*, 2001, 99, mid-page).

As mentioned previously, there are a multitude of therapies and treatments that are available, some involving conventional medical treatments, and others involving varying degrees of alternative treatment including, some from non-Western medical traditions. Any therapy is useful as long as it is not injurious, and enables the student to make progress in unblocking his or her mind and body in order to play better and remove those personal difficulties that stand in the way of successful audition and performance. Some of these treatments may be mental, psychological, physical, or various combinations of these. Blockages inhabit each student in varying degrees of mental, psychological, or physical ways, so no two treatment patterns will be alike. Treatments are highly individual (Greene, *Audition Success*, 2001, 84).

I know from personal experience that it is entirely possible to move from the high-anxious group to the low-anxious group and have a successful career as a result.

FINAL NOTES

One final subject I would like to touch on is the role of natural ability and genetics in musical performance. Without basic natural coordination, intelligence and the physical features necessary, it is true that one cannot reach the highest levels of musical refinement. If one is a brass player, a healthy body, lips, lungs and diaphragm, for breathing, and teeth that are not too crooked are essential (Farkas, 1962, 65). Beyond these factors, much depends on the individual and how he or she responds to the home environment they were raised in, specifically, the attitude of the parents to the child's desire or aptitude for a career in music. Much also depends on the child's strength of will and desire to pursue such a rewarding, but demanding career.

From a personal standpoint, professional symphonic auditions are challenging enough, and it is challenging to achieve effective and artistic playing. Propranolol's ability to block peripheral β-receptors thereby modifying autonomic expression of situational phobias, (including stage fright) e.g., heart rate (HR) as well as potential central effects from CNS β-blockade contributes to a lackluster and uninspired performance. This drug was developed to treat hypertension (Goodman and Gilman, 2002, 254), not to treat stage fright. The fine motor coordination and emotional connection necessary to performing music in the most artistic way, at the highest level (Greene, 2001, p. 72-73) demands that the performer not be compromised by the effects of neurochemical blockade in his or her system.

THE NEW FIELD OF PSYCHONEUROMUSICOLOGY

The answer is to create a new field of study, which I will call *psychoneuromusicology*, devoted to the study of the conscious mind's ability to use mental control, the idea of the *auto-transmission* of neurotransmitting chemicals, like those used in a trance, and those used by Adolph Herseth, William Scarlett, and Arnold Jacobs of the Chicago Symphony Orchestra, to induce a Zen-like state while playing music at the highest levels. This state is one of euphoria and relaxation. It is a state in which one can only *play* (italics mine) (Panksepp, 1990, 53) and play well (Gallwey, n.d.). It is the achieving of this state that can lead musicians and their audience to only the highest and most inspirational levels of musical expression, a true spiritual experience that can only help to heal a troubled world.

APPENDIX

Chicago Symphony Orchestra audition tape instructions, 2002. Note that the instructions say that "tone quality will not be a major consideration." In my experience, this is exactly the factor that disappears with the severe stage fright of the high-anxious group. Tone quality is a key factor in determining overall musical quality.

It is in your best interest to prepare a tape that accurately represents your playing without any misleading editing or enhancement. Intonation, rhythm, technique, and general musicality will be judged. Although tone quality will not be a major consideration, you should prepare as sonically excellent a tape as possible.

Text courtesy of the Chicago Symphony Orchestra. Reprinted with permission.

GLOSSARY

Note: all the following terms and definitions are based on (Rothenberg and Chapman, 2001) unless noted otherwise. Numbers cited in parenthesis are page references.

Adrenal medulla. The inner part of the adrenal gland, that manufactures and secretes hormones to regulate the activity of various tissues (15).

Adrenaline. See epinephrine (15).

Adrenergic. Indicates some relationship with epinephrine and norepinephrine (15).

Axon. Long part of the nerve cell process that carries impulse to site of action or response (59).

β-blockade. The process of blocking beta receptors. See beta adrenergic antagonist (68).

β1 and β2 receptors. One of two versions of structures in cell surface that receives both endogenous and exogenous substances. (15, 479). β receptors inhibit neurologic and hormonal responses. α receptors excite neurologic response. β1 are found in the heart, β2 are found in the lungs, blood vessels, and kidneys (Gringauz, 1997, 394).

Beta adrenergic antagonist. Substance that "blocks" or inhibits the action of the beta receptors described above (Ibid.).

Beta adrenergic receptor. See β1 and β2 receptors. Beta receptors that interact in some manner with epinephrine and norepinephrine (15).

Beta blocker. See beta adrenergic antagonist (68).

Boutons. Bulblike expansion at the tip of nerve axon (82).

Catecholamines. Any of the following group of chemicals produced in the adrenal medulla or in nervous tissue: epinephrine, dopamine, and norepinephrine (104).

Dendrite. A branching, treelike process that sends messages to the nerve cell body (153).

Dystonia. Abnormal muscle tone. The word is used here to denote weakened muscle due to overuse (173).

Effectors. Tissues that respond to nerve stimulation (Hoffmann).

Endogenous. Arising from within the body (189).

Epinephrine. A member of the group of catecholamines. Hormone of the adrenal medulla (104, 195). Also known by its alternative name, adrenaline (15).

Exogenous. Originating from outside the body (203).

Hyperventilation. Excessive breathing in excess of what the body needs (274).

Hypertension. Abnormally high blood pressure (273).

INDERAL®. Trade name for prescription drug, propranolol. (Goodman and Gilman, 2001, 253).

Muscle tremor. Involuntary rhythmic, quivering or shaking movements of the muscles (563).

Neurochemical blockade. Drug-induced condition in which the action of neurotransmitters are attenuated (Hoffmann).

Neuroeffector junction. Junction between nerve terminal and muscle or gland effector (Hoffmann).

Neuron. A nerve cell (389).

Neurotransmitters. Chemicals that transmit nerve impulses across synapses or neuroeffector junctions (390).

Norepinephrine. A member of the group of catecholamines. Hormone of the adrenal medulla. Also a neurotransmitter (104, 390, 395).

Peripheral nervous system. The peripheral nervous system is a network of nerves that extends to all the extremities of the body (433).

Performance anxiety. See definition for stage fright.

Presynaptic nerve terminals. Bouton-like structures at the end of nerve axons (Hoffmann). See bouton, axon.

Propranolol. Beta adrenergic antagonist, beta blocker, that blocks both $\beta 1$ and $\beta 2$ receptors "with equal affinity" (Goodman and Gilman, 2001, 253). See beta adrenergic antagonist.

Receptor terminals. Structures in cell surfaces that interact with both endogenous and exogenous chemicals (479).

Stage fright. A nervous and physiological condition in which normally competent functioning necessary for successful completion of the task at hand is impaired. It is also sometimes referred to as performance anxiety (Greene, *Fight Your Fear and Win*, 2001, vi).

Synapse. "In view, therefore, of the probable importance physiologically of this mode of nexus between neurone and neurone it is convenient to have a term for it. The term introduced has been *synapse*." (Sherrington, 1906, 17). Note: neurone is an alternate spelling for neuron. They refer to the same thing (Webster, 568).

Synaptic cleft. The anatomic "gap" across which nerve impulses are transmitted by neurotransmitters (Eccles, 1990, 3774).

SELECTED BIBLIOGRAPHY

Cameron, Julia. *The Artist's Way*. New York: G. Putnam's Sons.,1992.

Caruso, Enrico and Tetrazzini, Luisa. *Caruso and Tetrazzini on the Art of Singing*. New York: Dover Publications, Inc.,1975.

Clynes, Manfred, ed., *Music, Mind, and Brain: The Neuropsychology of Music*. New York and London: Plenum Press, 1982.

Copland, Aaron. *What to Listen for in Music*. New York: Mentor Books, 1953.

Doherty, Jim, "For All Who Crave a Horn That Thrills, This Bud's for You." *Smithsonian* 25, no. 6 (September 1994): 94-103.

Eccles, John C., "Developing Concepts of the Synapses." *The Journal of Neuroscience* 10 (12) (December 1990): 3769-3781.

Farkas, Philip. *The Art of Brass Playing*. Ann Arbor, MI: Edwards Bros., Inc., 1962 (for illustrations).

Frederiksen, Brian. *Arnold Jacobs: Song and Wind*. Wildwood, IL: WindSong Press, Ltd., 1996.

Fredrikson, Mats and Robert Gunnarsson. "Psychobiology of stage fright: The effect of public performance on neuroendocrine, cardiovascular, and subjective reactions." *Biological Psychology* 33 (1992):51-61.

Gallwey, Timothy. *The Inner Game of Confidence*. Read by the author. Windstar, n.d., Cassette.

Gladwell, Malcolm. "Performance Studies: The Art of Failure: Why Some People Choke and Others Panic." *New Yorker* (August 21 and 28), 2000.

Greene, Don. *Audition Success*. New York: Routledge, 2001.

Greene, Don. *Fight Your Fear and Win*. New York: Broadway Books, 2001.

Greene, Don. *Performance Success*. New York: Routledge,
          2002.

Gringauz, Alex. *Introduction to Medicinal Chemistry: How
          Drugs Act and Why*. New York: Wiley, 1997. (For Glossary
          entries).

Hadley, Benjamin, ed., *Britannica Book of Music*. Garden
          City, NY: Doubleday/Britannica Books, 1980.

Hardman, Joel G., Lee E. Limbard, and Alfred Goodman
          Gilman, eds., *Goodman and Gilman's The Pharmaceutical Basis
          of Therapeutics*, 10th ed. New York: McGraw-Hill, 2001.

Herseth, Adolph. "ITG Interview With Adolph Herseth."
          Interview by Michael Tunnell. *International Trumpet Guild
          Journal* (February 1999): 5-26.

Herseth, Adolph. Mike Goode's Private and Civic Orchestra Lessons
          with Adolph Herseth, 1994-2000, 4 volumes. Mike Goode's
          notes on Bud Herseth teaching Mike Goode and others the
          trumpet. Mike Goode's Private Collection, 1994-2000.

Hoffmann, Philip C. Class lectures at the University of
          Chicago, Gleacher Center, Chicago, Illinois, Spring
          Quarter, 2000. Mike Goode, transcriber, 3 vols.

Jacobs, Arnold. Arnold Jacobs' Summer Masterclass at
          Northwestern University, July 18-22, 1994. Mike Goode's
          notes from the lectures given by the author.
          Mike Goode's Private Collection, Oak Park, Illinois.

Jacobs, Arnold. Mike Goode's Lessons With Arnold Jacobs,
          1994-1996. Arnold Jacobs teaches Mike Goode the trumpet.
          Mike Goode's Private Collection, 1994-1996. 10 cassettes.

Jahn, Anthony, M.D. "Vocal Health: Well-Being, Q & A
          Allergies and Vocal Cysts." *Classical Singer* (October 1999): 11.

Lanier, Mike. Discussions with Mike Lanier, Principal
          Trumpet of the Evanston Symphony Orchestra. Mike Goode's
          conversations with Mike Lanier. Oak Park, IL: 2002.

Lavatelli, Celia Stendler. *Piaget's Theory Applied to an Early Childhood Curriculum.* Boston: American Science and Engineering, 1970.

Lee, Joseph Giam. Conversations with Joseph Lee about health, balance, and wellness from a Traditional Chinese Medicine Practitioner's perspective. Westmont, IL: Mike Goode, interviewer, 2002.

Neidig, Kenneth L. "'Man Alive, What a Kick This Is!' " An interview with Adolph "Bud" Herseth." *The Instrumentalist,* (April 1977): 38-44.

Panksepp, Jack. "A Role for Affective Neuroscience in Understanding Stress: The Case of Separation Distress Circuitry." In *Psychobiology of Stress,* Stefano Puglisi-Allegra, and Alberto Oliverio, eds., Dordrecht, Netherlands: Kluwer Academic Publishers, 1990: 41-57.

Parkland College. Conversations with former military band members in the Parkland Community College Band. Mike Goode's conversations with the members. Champaign, IL: 1994.

_____. *The Physician's Desk Reference,* 54ᵗʰ ed., Montvale, New Jersey: Medical Economics Co., Inc., 2002.

Rothenberg, Mikel A., and Charles F. Chapman. *Dictionary of Medical Terms for the Nonmedical Person.,* 4ᵗʰ ed. Hauppauge, NY: Barron's Educational Series, 2000.

Scarlett, William. Mike Goode's Lessons With William Scarlett, 2000-2002, 5 volumes. William Scarlett teaches Mike Goode the trumpet. Mike Goode's private collection, 1999-2002.

Scholes, Percy A. *The Concise Oxford Dictionary of Music.* London: Oxford University Press, 1952.

Sherrington, Charles S. *The Integrative Action of the Nervous System.* New York: Charles Scribner's Sons, 1906.

Smith, Philip. *Orchestral Excerpts for Trumpet With Spoken Commentary, Philip Smith, Principal Trumpet New York Philharmonic.* Summit Records DCD 144, n.d. Compact disc.

Walter, Bruno. *The Art of Conducting: Great Conductors of the
        Past.* Interview with Bruno Walter. Devised by
        Stephen Wright, directed by Sue Knussen, 117 minutes,
        Teldec Video, 1994, videocassette.

_____. Webster's New Collegiate Dictionary, 7th
        ed., s.v. "neuron."

Wolfe, James. Conversations with James Wolfe, Elementary
        School Band Director, East Maine School District No. 63. Niles,
        IL: East Maine School District No. 63, 1964.

Zouves, Maria. "The Joy of Singing: A Conversation with
        Dame Joan Sutherland." *Classical Singer* (October 1999): 6-7,
        14.

APPENDIX TO THE SECOND EDITION

Note: This was originally written for my graduate class "Regulation of Human Physiological Systems (Homeostasis)" at the University of Chicago in the Spring of 2000. It was taught by Philip C. Hoffmann who later became my thesis advisor.

PHYSIOLOGICAL EFFECTS OF REBREATHING OF CO2 IN TRUMPET-PLAYING

BY MICHAEL I. GOODE

Most of us take the physiological process of breathing for granted. Only if we are unlucky enough to become afflicted with a severe respiratory disease will most of us be forced to think twice about the physiological process involved.

When we inhale air, this air is normally higher in oxygen (O2) than the air that has just been exhaled which is higher in carbon dioxide (CO2). The outside air that we inhale is brought into the lungs by its air sacs, the alveoli. These air sacs, through the process of diffusion, exchange the newly received oxygen for carbon dioxide received from the circulatory system. The carbon dioxide is exhaled through ventilation of the lungs into the outside air. The entire process is regulated by the pons-medulla of the brain and so is not normally under conscious control.[1] Both respiration and the kidneys help regulate the normal homeostatic balance of carbon dioxide and oxygen in the blood. This balance can be expressed as the slightly akaline pH number of 7.4.

Although we are normally consciously unaware of this breathing process and the physiological aspects of it, there are instances in which healthy individuals choose to think about and have conscious control of their breathing. Speaking, singing, and playing a wind instrument are some examples of conscious control of breathing. These persons belong to the class of "voluntary breathing acts," in contrast to *involuntary breathing* which we discussed previously as being controlled by the pons-medulla.[2]

Even though there are many physiological aspects to the process of conscious control of breathing, we are going to limit ourselves to the discussion of voluntary breathing acts involving the playing of wind instruments rather than those acts that concern singing or speaking. We are also going to talk only of physiological factors relating to the balance of oxygen and carbon dioxide that relate to respiration and their effects. Space limitations prevent us from further discussion of other physiological aspects concerning the playing of wind instruments and respiration other than what is needed for clarity.

A wind instrument, such as a trumpet, relies on vibrations of the lips in a cup-shaped mouthpiece, which create sound waves.[3] These sound waves are amplified through some 1.4 m of brass tubing and are finally projected outwards through a funnel-shaped device at the end of the instrument known as the bell (Fig. 9).[4]

The playing of such an instrument requires much larger amounts of air and different breathing techniques than does normal respiration in a healthy individual. Those who play such instruments must think about how they are breathing.[5] Much conscious training is initially involved in learning the mechanics of breathing in a wind instrument.[6] The student must learn to inhale from the corners of the mouth with varying degrees of speed and intensity.

These differing degrees of speed and intensity can be measured with standard medical respiratory devices such as the Voldyne® and Inspiron, which are normally used for respiratory rehabilitation purposes in a postoperative recovery situation.[7]

By the time the student reaches the professional level, the mastery of breathing techniques becomes essential.[8] In orchestral playing, long passages of sufficient duration can be handled with ease through the mastery of proper breathing mechanics. Mastery of these breathing mechanics is adequate for most wind instruments; however, it is not always sufficient for instruments of the brass family. These instruments are required, at times, in large orchestras to sustain long passages at very loud volumes reaching 120 dB or more.

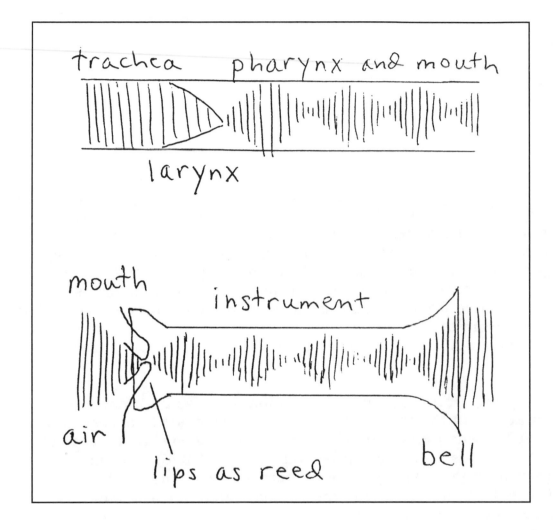

Fig. 9. Generation of sound waves in the larynx and in the trumpet (bottom). From Bouhuys, Arend. *The Physiology of Breathing: A Textbook for Medical Students*, New York: Grune & Stratton, 1977, p. 267, Figure 11-1. Original diagram adapted by Michael I. Goode. Adapted and reprinted by permission of Grune & Stratton, Inc.

A professional trumpeter requires highly specialized training to be able to voluntarily play his or her instrument with an airflow and pressure rate similar to that of the tuba.[9] This highly specialized training enables the trumpet player to produce a very large resonant sound that is uncharacteristic of most people's perception of the instrument. This training is necessary in a very large orchestra, such as the Chicago Symphony, in order to be able to play one's part at loud volumes for a sustained period of time. The works of Gustav Mahler and Richard Strauss for example, require this type of sustained playing.

The rapid inhalation and exhalation of oxygen (O2) and carbon dioxide (CO2) make it nearly impossible in these situations to avoid the phenomenon of hyperventilation. It is only through the rebreathing of carbon dioxide through the instrument that the effect of hyperventilation can be brought under control as I will explain in this paper. The rebreathing also brings the body back into homeostasis.[10] In normal respiration, oxygen is inhaled and carbon dioxide is exhaled as a result of the exchange process that takes place in the alveoli in the lungs. Through the process of diffusion, CO2 is carried from the blood cells through the interstitial milieu that lies between the alveoli and the individual blood cells. At the same time, oxygen diffuses across the blood cell walls into the intracellular milieu.[11]

This is the routine exchange process that occurs in normal respiration. In hyperventilation, the carbon dioxide level goes down as can be measured by the pressure of the CO2 level that enters the alveolus. This pressure can be notated as PCO2.[12] Also, in hyperventilation, the oxygen level increases, and this can be measured by the pressure of the O2 that enters the alveolus. Oxygen pressure can be notated in a similar way to the alveolar carbon dioxide pressure described earlier as PO2.[13]

The resultant change in the levels of alveolar carbon dioxide and oxygen cause the alveolar environment to be more alkaline, a condition called alkalinotosis.[14] This can be graphically illustrated by the Rahn and Fenn diagram (See Fig.10).[15] The diagram shows the changes in the acid-base relationship for voluntary hyperventilation.

As experienced through personal experiment and observation as a professional trumpeter in large symphony orchestras, the author posits that this condition occurs not just in high-airflow low-pressure

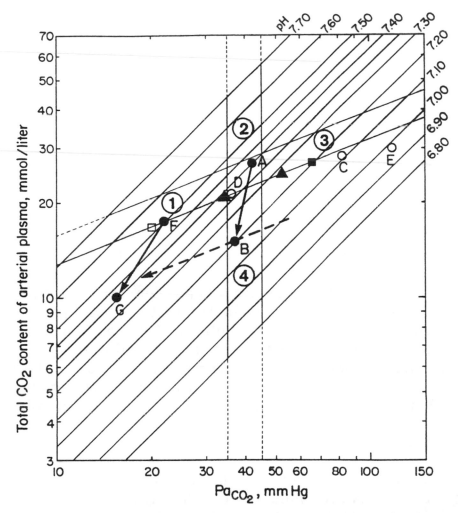

Fig. 6-19. This and the following figures use the Peters diagram [83] for a graphical assessment of changes in acid-base status. Pa_{CO_2} (abscissa) and $[CO_2]$ of arterial plasma are plotted on log scales. Hence, lines for equal pH run at a 45° angle in the diagram (see Eq. 5, p. 126). Range of normal pH values is indicated by shading between the pH lines for pH = 7.35 and for pH = 7.45. Range of normal Pa_{CO_2} values (35–45 mm Hg) is indicated by the vertical gray area. Two upward sloping lines enclosing another gray area are CO_2 dissociation curves. Lower one of these is the same as the curve for fully oxygenated blood in Fig. 6-16. Upper CO_2 dissociation curve is parallel to the lower one; in the range of normal P_{CO_2} and pH, it indicates the upper limits of normal $[CO_2]$ (approx. 28 mmol/liter).

Areas designated by circled numbers *1* to *4* represent respiratory alkalosis (*1*), nonrespiratory alkalosis (*2*), respiratory acidosis (*3*), and nonrespiratory acidosis (*4*). Specific data points are as follows: ▲: points A_2 and A_3 in Fig. 5-4, p. 85; □: acute hyperventilation; ■: breath holding after O_2 inspiration.[86] Arrow *AB*: average control (*A*) and postexercise data points in healthy athletes.[16] Arrow *FG*: acute respiratory alkalosis on first exposure to high altitude (*F*), followed by compensation during altitude acclimatization (to *G*). Data from Rahn and Fenn.[86] ○: (*C, D, E*): three data points obtained over a 15-hour period in a patient with intermittent acute respiratory acidosis (p. 138 in ref. 73). Dashed arrow through *B*—see text for explanation.

Fig. 10. Rahn and Fenn data done on a Peters diagram. From Bouhuys, Arend, *The Physiology of Breathing: A Textbook for Medical Students*, New York: Grune & Stratton., 1977, p.134, Reprinted by permission of Grune & Stratton, Inc.

instruments like the tuba[16] *but also in the trumpet when played in a similar fashion* with high airflow and low pressure as discussed previously in this paper. Playing the trumpet in this manner as we have said before causes hyperventilation.

Such hyperventilation if sustained can cause serious damage to not only the respiratory system, but also to the body in general.[17] The alkaline condition in both the lungs and the body must be resolved in order to bring the body back into homeostasis. Prolonged respiratory alkalosis with a pH greater than 7.45 can turn into a condition that is very damaging to the body known as acute respiratory alkalosis.[18] This is resolved by somehow introducing more carbon dioxide back into the body to bring the pH back to its normal level of 7.4.[19]

The simple way that the player can solve this problem is by rebreathing the exhaled air through his instrument[20] by placing his lips around the mouthpiece as he or she inhales. This action enables him or her to take advantage of the fact that the air within the instrument is already higher in its percentage of carbon dioxide than the outside air. Inhaling this air automatically raises the percentage of carbon dioxide in the alveolus. This inhalation causes the alveolar pressure of CO_2 to rise to a sufficient level so that the body comes closer to its normal pH of 7.4.

Repeated rebreathing of the CO_2-rich air in the instrument is done until the body is put back into homeostasis. Physical symptoms associated with hyperventilation, such as dizziness and loss of mental function, also disappear once homeostasis is achieved.[21] Although this may seem like a simple solution, it is effective and accomplishes its job of keeping the body in balance. The feeling of well-being associated with the return of homeostatic balance is not lost upon the player. The resumption of a feeling of well-being enables the player to now concentrate on the task at hand. The ability to concentrate is one of the key factors in the highly stressful career of professional orchestral trumpet playing.

Also, the player has taken a step, through rebreathing, to ensure the safety of his or her health by the prevention of prolonged hyperventilation and its possible deleterious health effects.

ENDNOTES

[1] Hoffmann, Philip C. Class lecture at the University of Chicago, Gleacher Center, Chicago, Illinois, May 24, 2000. Mike Goode, transcriber.

[2] Bouhuys, Arend. *The Physiology of Breathing: A Textbook for Medical Students*. New York: Grune & Stratton., 1977, 286.

[3] Bouhuys, 267.

[4] World Book, 2000 ed., s.v. "Trumpet".

[5] Bouhuys, 266.

[6] Frederiksen, Brian, 1996. *Arnold Jacobs: Song and Wind.* Edited by John Taylor. Gurnee, Illinois: Windsong Press, Ltd. , 101-103.

[7] Frederiksen, 178, 181.

[8] Ibid, 91.

[9] Bouhuys, 282.

[10] Frederiksen, 110.

[11] Hoffmann, Philip C. Class lecture, at the University of Chicago, Gleacher Center, Chicago, Illinois, April 12, 2000. Mike Goode, transcriber.

[12] Bouhuys, 251.

[13] Ibid.

[14] Ibid.

[15] Bouhuys, 134.

[16] Frederiksen, 110, and Bouhuys, 282.

17 Hoffmann, Philip C. Class lecture.

18 Bouhuys, 137.

19 Frederiksen, 110.

20 Ibid.

21 Ibid.

INDEX